CONCILIUM

Religion in the Eighties

CONCILIUM

Editorial Directors

Giuseppe Alberigo	Bologna	Italy
Gregory Baum	Toronto	Canada
Leonardo Boff	Petrópolis	Brazil
Antoine van den Boogaard	Nijmegen	The Netherlands
Paul Brand	Ankeveen	The Netherlands
Marie-Dominique Chenu OP	Paris	France
John Coleman SJ	Berkeley, Ca.	USA
Mary Collins OSB	Washington	USA
Yves Congar OP	Paris	France
Mariasusai Dhavamony SJ	Rome	Italy
Christian Duquoc OP	Lyon	France
Virgil Elizondo	San Antonio, Texas	USA
Casiano Floristán	Madrid	Spain
Claude Geffré OP	Paris	France
Norbert Greinacher	Tübingen	West Germany
Gustavo Gutiérrez	Lima	Peru
Peter Huizing SJ	Nijmegen	The Netherlands
Bas van Iersel SMM	Nijmegen	The Netherlands
Jean-Pierre Jossua OP	Paris	France
Hans Küng	Tübingen	West Germany
Nicholas Lash	Cambridge	Great Britain
René Laurentin	Paris	France
Johannes-Baptist Metz	Münster	West Germany
Dietmar Mieth	Düdingen	Switzerland
Jürgen Moltmann	Tübingen	West Germany
Roland Murphy OCarm	Durham, NC	USA
Jacques Pohier OP	Paris	France
David Power OMI	Washington, DC	USA
Karl Rahner SJ	Munich	West Germany
Luigi Sartori	Padua	Italy
Edward Schillebeeckx OP	Nijmegen	The Netherlands
Elisabeth Schüssler Fiorenza	Hyattsville, Ind.	USA
David Tracy	Chicago	USA
Knut Walf	Nijmegen	The Netherlands
Anton Weiler	Nijmegen	The Netherlands
John Zizioulas	Glasgow	Great Britain

Lay Specialist Advisers

José Luis Aranguren	Madrid/Santa Barbara, Ca.	Spain/USA
Luciano Caglioti	Rome	Italy
August Wilhelm von Eiff	Bonn	West Germany
Paulo Freire	Perdizes, São Paulo	Brazil
Harald Weinrich	Munich	West Germany

Concilium 165 (5/1983): Fundamental Theology

BT
33
I52
v.165

INDIFFERENCE
TO
RELIGION

Edited by
Jean-Pierre Jossua
and
Claude Geffré

English Language Editor
Marcus Lefébure

WITHDRAWN

T. & T. CLARK LTD
Edinburgh

THE SEABURY PRESS
New York

HIEBERT LIBRARY
Fresno Pacific College - M. B. Seminary
Fresno, Calif. 93702

21934

Copyright © 1983, by Stichting Concilium, T. & T. Clark Ltd and The Seabury Press
Inc. All rights reserved. Nothing contained in this publication shall be multiplied and/or
made public by means of print, photographic print, microfilm, or in any other manner
without the previous written consent of the Stichting Concilium, Nijmegen (Holland),
T. & T. Clark Ltd, Edinburgh (Scotland) and The Seabury Press Inc., New York
(USA).

May 1983
T. & T. Clark Ltd, 36 George Street, Edinburgh EH2 2LQ
ISBN: 0 567 30845 5

The Seabury Press, 815 Second Avenue, New York, NY 10017
ISBN: 0 8164 2445 4

Library of Congress Catalog Card No.: 82—062758

Printed in Scotland by William Blackwood & Sons Ltd, Edinburgh

Concilium: Monthly except July and August.
Subscriptions 1983: UK and Rest of the World £27·00, postage and handling included;
USA and Canada, all applications for subscriptions and enquiries about *Concilium*
should be addressed to The Seabury Press, 815 Second Avenue, New York, NY 10017,
USA.

CONTENTS

Part III
Bulletins

Editorial

WHAT IS the meaning of the religious indifference Christians are running up against on such a massive scale? Is it mainly practical: materialism, a lack of attention paid to the fundamental questions of existence and the search for God? Or should it be regarded as a long-term consequence of considered atheism or agnosticism: have they had the time to work out a less polemical attitude towards religions than that formed at the outset, which was anything but indifferent? Should we not have the broadmindedness to read it as the reverse side of the attainment of the essentially positive values of human maturity and autonomy, but involving as price to be paid this possibly temporary oversight?

And to begin with, is the situation the same everywhere? The discussions of the board of directors of *Concilium* on this project, as on the subject of other plans for issues considered in previous years, have revealed such different climates of opinion that the theologians present seemed no longer even to understand one another. The 'remnant', what remains after the collapse of unanimous beliefs of politico-religious Christianity, is apparently by no means the same everywhere. It can be near zero—religious unbelief and total indifference—in one country, and elsewhere attest to very concentrated popular religiousness (itself of widely varying significance—in Italy or Brazil, for example—but this is not the place to go into that), or again as a sort of theist consensus that is vague enough. One of our major concerns in the preparation of this issue was therefore to obtain contributions from authors capable of describing the different contexts.

Our intention here would not be to tackle modern 'unbelief' in a global way, with all its typical forms, but solely religious indifference, in order to attempt to analyse it in a more concise way. We are well aware that when this subject is raised at present it is the done thing to show an eagerness—in particular in Christian milieux—to take into account a 'return to the religious life', a renewal of interest which is countering it more or less everywhere. Even if we suppose that this phenomenon is not being grossly exaggerated and that it co-exists in the same area as indifference (and not in other countries, or in other social groups, or quite simply in a Christian milieu), it does not diminish at all the importance of what we are analysing, which in our opinion is by no means on the decrease. Whatever the case, another issue of the journal appearing this year, on the sociology of religion, deals with the new forms of religiousness and renewals of religious motivation. Thus we did not have to compensate here for the possibly unilateral nature of our subject: the two issues should be taken as a whole, without of course guaranteeing agreement of everything published in the journal!

The first part represents an attempt at mapping out guidelines and diagnosis, in several different contexts. We asked Fr Jacques Sommet, the director in France of the 'Unbelief-Faith Service', to try to evaluate the breadth of the phenomenon and in particular to identify the different types, a fundamental operation in a cultural milieu as complex as that of the French, Latin or West German, paying particular attention to the young, whose unbelief is rapidly assuming massive proportions. After a brief historical survey, he offers an illuminating classification, sensitive to everything that there may be of value behind religious unbelief—a too negative term. For the Anglo-Saxon world, where social religion and a sort of diffuse religiosity modify the picture very markedly, we have asked for another study from Robert Kress, requesting him, on the prompting of correspondents, to examine in detail those persons or groups to whom the epithet of 'religious' should be applied. In fact, he suggests from the outset a utilisable definition of the term 'religion'—which a French author would doubtless beware of doing—and quite precise criteria for differentiating between religious indifference and interest; he then draws an interesting picture of the situation in the USA. Thirdly, we thought it necessary to study one particularly emphatic form of indifference, placed in a context other than that of the post-Christian world: this is what Joseph Spae's generous analysis supplies. He seems on the whole to find value in the religious search which remains at the heart of the detachment which the Japanese have in regard to traditional religions. Finally, we wanted a more global article, half-way between evidence and judgment, where an attempt is made to distinguish the recognisable factors in the rapid worsening of religious indifference in the West. We would suggest roughly: the link with the affluent society, the discrediting of the institutional churches and of their authorities, the broader context of the indifference of people today with regard to the most fundamental questions of meaning, the popularisation of modern criticisms of religion, the consequences of an improved knowledge of the diversity of religions. Our colleague A. Weiler has given us a remarkable historical survey and a profound analysis of the present situation.

The second part comprises three attempts at interpretation. We consider ourselves very fortunate in obtaining Dr Obrist's interesting contribution. Nevertheless, we would first like to say a word about the original plan, which has not been realised here. A critical elucidation seemed essential to us: a 'religious' recovery of the non-religious is constantly being attempted, which is ultimately apologetic; for example, a definition of the 'religious' person is made which is so inclusive that it masks the problem of massive-scale indifference; or again, the symbols of the substitution are declared religious, whereas non-religious approaches to the absolute exist. Nevertheless, the possibility should be recognised of an authentic spiritual and perhaps even mystical human life, without religion! Whatever the case, W. Obrist has suggested to us a profound reflection on religious indifference as a symptom of the alteration of the modern consciousness: demythologisation of nature and history, a revolution which is represented by the new perception of the matter-spirit duality. There still are people whose indifference is marked by positivism, but there are already others who, beyond that mutation, are in reality beings in quest of religion who have not managed to discover a proposition untrammelled by archaism. And we have put to A. R. Schlette a question which preoccupies us: these men and women who are 'indifferent'—are they absolutely so? What sort of interest, appetite, desire, openness towards the question of God or evangelical witness do they still have? Why do many of them refuse to be characterised as 'unbelievers'? What does positive agnosticism mean: a sympathy which does not have an object? Without answering all these questions, he has tried to clear the field by distinguishing between indifference and conscious agnosticism, by analysing the transition from one to the other—which he finds an advance—and by evaluating the relations between agnosticism and religion, which are much more profound and positive than is generally thought. To conclude this section, Claude Geffré examines the status of the faith in this unprecedented situation of the decline of religion. After a new effort at understanding and gauging the latter, he shows that a post-atheist faith is subjected to a critical trial, invited to a reinterpretation, tested by deep-seated division, faced with the absence of God in the world. This is why its adherence to God is gratuitous in nature, beyond the utilitarian representations and the social functions of God.

Three 'bulletins' will conclude this issue. Men and women find the path of faith in this situation of indifference—why? On what conditions? In presenting to us the progress of the faith and of the Church in a popular milieu, the Cardinal Cardijn seminary, I. Berten attempts to clarify the second of these two questions. And Jean Collet makes a remarkable analysis of the presence of indifference in the audio-visual field and indifference with regard to images, a broader indifference than that which concerns religion, but which helps to situate the latter. Finally, Rosino Gibellini has very opportunely suggested that we take into account in this issue the dossier on religious indifference from the 'Secretariat for non-believers' of Rome. We hope that all these contributions, inevitably fragmentary and not claiming to cover the whole ground of the problem raised, will prove as illuminating to our readers as they were to ourselves.

JEAN-PIERRE JOSSUA
CLAUDE GEFFRÉ

Translated by Della Couling

PART I

An Attempted Diagnosis

Jacques Sommet

Religious Indifference Today:
A Draft Diagnosis

THESE LINES are not intended as a comprehensive diagnosis of religious indifference at the present time. They are simply meant to open up the field for the articles which follow, and which all form part of this joint enterprise.

Nothing is more difficult than trying to land on the shores of a continent with a very ancient history. Moreover, the starting-point we choose must be one which leaves us open to the documents which follow this introduction. We shall therefore present some silhouettes and significant situations, in the knowledge that the sequel will show whether they are solid or unreliable.

Religious indifference is certainly a characteristic feature of European society, and perhaps of that of the whole world, at the present time. If we are to speak about it, we must first set it in the context of its origins and developments. Two lines of approach will help us in this task: a provisional definition, a kind of hypothesis from which to start out; and an analysis in depth which may form a basis on which the outlines of indifferences can be drawn—that is to say, the state of unbelief today, along with the tools which may be used for its analysis. After that we shall attempt a typology, as concrete as possible, of religious indifference as a sign of our times.

Religious indifference can be provisionally described in the following terms: first of all, this indifference gives the immediate impression of being 'a lack of interest in the question of God, or of his involvement or representation in daily life'. It should be understood that the question of God here embraces any sense of responsibility a man may feel in response to an unconditional and basic call, for which no name has yet been found—a situation in which the person 'called' may not yet know the 'caller', the origin and foundation of his liberty. Anyone involved in a quest of that kind is certainly not in a state of indifference, even if the word God finds no place in his vocabulary. He is one who 'is looking for meaning'. It is lack of interest in such a quest which constitutes religious indifference. We shall look at this question in relation to the history of atheism, of unbelief, and of faith, preliminary stages in the approach to our basic subject.

1. OUR HISTORY: THREE PREPARATORY STAGES OF CONTEMPORARY INDIFFERENCE

(a) A denial of the existence of God, in the name of a certain kind of reason, may lie behind indifference, but it is not to be confused with it. In Europe, since the sixteenth century, and especially in the eighteenth and nineteenth centuries, the influence of the philosophy of the Enlightenment, the *Aufklärung*, has concentrated attention on man as the *agent of progress*, in the ever more clearly defined context of an evolutionistic positivism. Thence comes the objection to religion, and especially 'the Christian system', the forms of which seem to express either the domination of the social groups actually in power, or the imaginary nature of the unreal world, dreamed about and projected into the hoped-for future by those suffering from a fundamental alienation, in either the rural world or the developing industrial world. This first period is characterised by the establishment of atheism as the struggle against every religious ideology, and later by the substitution of an ideology directed against every kind of religious faith. This positive ideology is scientific atheism in that it represents the struggle of reason, militant atheism by virtue of its activity. It is necessary at one and the same time to establish the reign of reason as the normal practice, and to bring about the destruction of the opposition, those who believe, as a group with a reciprocal right to exist.[1] The way to anticlericalism and fanaticism is then open.

This stage, however, was not to prove decisive. From the nineteenth century onwards there have been examples of scientific progress and liberty co-existing alongside faith, in individuals—for example, discoverers such as Pasteur or Branly—and also in clearly worked out, even militant, philosophical positions—as in the case of Buchez, for example. It is true that *scientific* and *militant* atheism has for a long time been mounting a struggle against religion, as representing oppression and delusion. At the same time, those involved in political life from the Christian side have claimed that liberty is a sign of the Christian vocation itself. Lacordaire, among others, is a striking example of this.

(*b*) Another period now begins—one in which *violence* and *technical and scientific efficiency* make necessary a fresh analysis of society. This involves calling into question the opposition between atheism and the religious system. Up to that point atheism had denied any possible human meaning to whatever admitted any kind of faith. To affirm God was to deny man. From the other side, the believer was unable to accept that a non-believer could be a man in the deepest sense. But it happened that two global catastrophes (1914-1918 and 1939-1945) sprang up out of the ground prepared by atheistic rationality and the Christian system. Subsequently there have been social and cultural upheavals which have called into question both religion and critical reason. Those who formerly were convinced atheists or dogmatic believers have had to trust each other and combine their efforts to build a future which lies beyond their denials or affirmations. They are having to judge each other and help each other in the light of their active hope in the future, across the confrontation—sometimes difficult, sometimes positive—of the *attitudes* and *convictions*[2] of faith or unbelief, out beyond their prior and exclusive 'credos'. Not that faith, or religion, have become credible in themselves. Marx, Freud and Nietzsche can still evoke the suspicion that every expression of Christian faith is the illusive effect of religion combined with various forms of domination. Nevertheless the Frankfurt School, the last stage in the development of theoretical and critical Marxism in Germany, has ended up, paradoxically, with a 'nostalgia' for an absolute foundation, necessary and impossible at the same time, for communication between the liberties.

Thus this second stage, having developed in the way we have shown, ends with a transformation which is of decisive significance for the future. A new society has grown up in the midst of this violence, which began in Europe but has become global, and it is exploding into a transformed universe. This new world has several characteristic features, of which the first is the widespread diffusion of *technology*. Technology, applied intensively, has determined the pattern of life for a great number of people, a pattern limited to verifiable results, repeated to the point at which boredom supervenes, despite the immense chances of survival which such technology brings. At all events, the method of applied science, at this stage, shows itself independent of any reference to religious faith, and leads to an overall rational indifference to the tradition of faith. It would seem that only a person's private life can remain under the influence of such faith.

But this society cannot be contained within the bounds of scientific and technical developments. The population of the whole world finds itself engaged in one single dramatic adventure. A second characteristic feature is *violence*, as new needs overtake the certainties and non-belief of the sciences, and question their rational basis. This does not, however, involve a return to religion, but rather a further shattering of it. The Christian 'city' now represents only a minority in the world. But at least the Church is gradually giving up its desire to dominate, and is becoming capable of collective initiatives for the benefit of human groups devastated by oppression and hunger. This is where the unbeliever can respect the believer, and vice versa. There has been an about-turn. The opposing parties have both lost part of their *dogmas* and their attachment to their *institutions*. They have opened their doors to people other than their own adherents. A *dialogue* has been set up on the common ground of human rights, for example. Away from their institutions and their petrified certainties, 'not very good believers' from the churches, and 'non-atheistic unbelievers' from the other side, are inaugurating a new phase of openness to a reciprocal and transforming exchange between unbelief and faith. Such is our present situation.

(c) Nevertheless, nothing is final. The positive encounter of the unbeliever and the believer leads, it is true, to dialogue. But elsewhere, too, where dialogue is not the order of the day, we find, in contrast, paradoxically, with our past, that the criticism *of reason by religion* is an accepted principle and an established fact. We refer here to 'socially visible' religion, in its somewhat ambiguous relationship to faith. In the vast expanse of Asia, from the Islam of Iraq or Iran to modern forms of Buddhism, religion as a social form is reasserting its right to be an effective force, by means of its control over the personal conscience. In such conditions, where it is a force established for political purposes, religion itself tends towards unbelief in its own forms of expression. The symbol acquires an arbitrary efficacity—as, for example, in the proclamation of holy wars! We see that in this case faith in the God of liberty is opposed to the religion of an entity such as nation or mobilised people, that it is opposed to power given the sanction of religion. But this distinction is clear only to a small number of believers in personal faith, or unbelievers with a respect for liberty. For most people, religion and reason practised in this way are simply a scandal. Hence the drift, for quite other reasons than in the technological context, from faith to unbelief, *from belief to indifference*, in the face of so many risks of alienation through politicised religion. This completes the picture in which can be seen, in their origins, the links between *atheism and religion*, then between *unbelief and faith*, and finally *of faith and unbelief in their opposition to the sacralised society*.

2. CONSCIOUS UNBELIEF TODAY

These historical stages have thus provided us with a geographical setting which is the prerequisite for understanding religious indifference. Against this background we can proceed to a description of current forms of conscious unbelief. This is our first concern. Only after that shall we be able to perceive that unbelief is absolute indifference, a total refusal in principle and in practice to ask questions—though we have seen that conscious unbelief does not always manage to avoid it. We shall then be able to grasp this widespread and very contemporary phenomenon of indifference in a more or less pure state, and make a proper religious analysis of our society.

The presence of unbelievers

Let us first recall that there are still people today who take the path of uncompromising negation, and so continue the rationalistic *atheism* of the nineteenth century. 'The Voice of Atheists' (*La Voix des athées*) has been more virulent than ever since 1976. The 'Atheism Liaison Committee' (CLA) embraces various groups, of which the well-known 'Rationalist Union' is sometimes one of the less rigorous in its denials (see note 1).

A different group is that of *negative agnostics*. The atheists to whom we were referring base themselves on 'certainties', but we are now dealing with 'the unbelief of uncertainty'. This is the world of the uneasy and suspicious, who are not prepared to take any steps to justify their attitude. People find themselves in this category through weariness, or simply lack of time. They are uncertain because they lack support, and they end up sometimes with a blind fidelity to dominant ideologies or to 'in' groups. Otherwise they pass over into total indifference. We shall return to this point.

But we have also to recognise around us a world which is perhaps very extensive, where there is a different kind of unbelief. It can be called the *universe of positive agnosticism*. By that we mean the universe of those whose uncertainty about God and the meaning of life takes the form of a quest which does not despise the searchings or the certainties of others, but does not copy them either.

These are the men and women who will be able to enter into dialogue among themselves and with all other searchers after meaning. They will often ask questions of those believers whose certainty is linked with a tradition, and who enjoy a freedom born of a Word of which they are not the origin. The 'Unbelief-Faith' dialogue thus constitutes one of the most profound and most thrilling adventures of our times. The profound dynamism of humanity 'in search of a meaning' develops through the basic solidarities established between people as a result of the interplay of these two poles of faith and non-faith. No conscious human being can escape it.

This finds expression, in every kind of situation, through structured attitudes, sometimes of a provisional nature, sometimes more permanent, which result from the balance between the open research of positive agnosticism on one side and faith on the other, and which together form *patterns of belief*.

These beliefs, which are neither true faith nor pure negation, are worked out through the tension between these two poles set up in a variety of situations. Sometimes they tend towards faith, with a recognition of a transcendent claim, while at other times they tend towards 'open' agnosticism. One person will refuse to deny God; another will experience the adventure of a nameless prayer, through the poetry of humility and hope; yet another will find he can be more true to himself by rejecting language about meaning, while not despising those who make use of the historical expressions of the believing community. Another, again, will rediscover himself in the individualism of pure rational thought, which is both demanding and critical. A fitting symbol of this adventure is the coming together of the two philosophers Blondel and Brunschvicg, who at the end of their lives found themselves united in the solidarity of misfortune. Let us then accept the combination of unbelief and faith, incorporating agnosticism of one type or another. With this unbelief-faith current flowing through them, *beliefs* may be such either in the minimal sense that they imply reference to a religious group, popular religions, or other kinds of groups, or they may be beliefs with a strong trust in the infinite quality of questionings about life.

This is how the outline of a universe 'in search of a meaning' may be drawn. So many men and women find themselves sharing a common life, with variations. But then there appears a new solidarity among all those to whom we have just been referring, a solidarity based on the fact that they cannot help sharing a common view of those who at this point fail to 'keep their appointment'. These people receive something unexpected from each other, but only on condition that they engage in dialogue. How then can they fail to have thoughts about those who exist like themselves but turn their back on those questions which are implicit in the unbelief-faith partnership, questions of living by beliefs, of looking for the meaning of life?

Here we find ourselves on the shore of an ocean which has no other sound than its murmur of humanity: the infinite, unbounded sea of religious indifference, of not searching for a meaning. Can we, in such a difficult dialogue, unravel the existence of this indifference, and locate its fate and its forms? It remains true that we, whether we are open unbelievers or believers, cannot escape from what such indifference lays before us: the question of the innumerable people who exist—and no more than that!

3. PATTERNS OF INDIFFERENCE AT THE PRESENT TIME

(a) The indifference of decay

Religious indifference begins simply with lack of interest in any kind of meaning life may have, here and now. But in order to be indifferent it is necessary to live, or at least to show some slight taste for living. According to Rosenzweig, living indifferently requires at the very least some reference to 'an original something'. However, at the level of empirical existence we often, in practice, come up against the 'so what?' of young or old. Is it worth the bother to think about some possible value? This suggests what might be called the *indifference of personal decay*, or of evasion, which may lead in the end to suicide, by way of alcohol, drugs, purposeless destruction, etc.

(b) The indifference of action and passion

Yet, overall, one must try to live. But then this ambition may be limited to the pursuit of a restricted and controlled goal. There is no place for open-minded research of the indeterminate or the infinite, nor yet for any message coming from elsewhere. Indifference is expressed here by the reference of every undertaking to 'an interest', here and now.

This interest involves action, but the action proposed is limited to what can be seized, attained, possessed. This is the *indifference of action*, consisting in the determined mastery of something partial and fragmentary.

Even within its limitations, however, this active type of indifference finds expression in steps of variable intensity. The attitude of a great part of society born of today's organisation conforms to a model very restrained in its definition of goals. The model can be defined by reference to a carefully calculated balance of the needs to be met. The men and women of the lower classes of the technological society work out very precisely their means of support. Nurses, or civil servants, are motivated in the management of their affairs by the desire to survive. The pursuit of a *happy security* absorbs their daily life. Nothing else exists, apart from a few transitory indulgences, an evanescent luxury (gambling games, betting on horses, a desire to know all the 'news'—sporting and otherwise—without running the risk of getting involved).

But this level of indifference does not satisfy all those who act out of interest. We come next to groups of people motivated by the *passion* to act in pursuit of a goal which, though not distant, is risky, and which closes every other opening. This is the *indifference of passion*, where there is an active search that is expressed in the blockage

B

constituted by the dominant desire either for an object (the collector), or for an activity (a group of motor cyclists, with their dangers and solidarities), or for some deeply-committed activity at the social level, which 'leaves no time' for anything else! At the extreme, the infinite aspect of the desire may almost break through the need to enjoy oneself, or to dominate others, by which a person is motivated, but it never succeeds in liberating itself. Finally this dynamic kind of indifference triumphs over every ultimate over-stepping of the mark, over all unconditioned human solidarity. Paths such as these, which are sometimes open to the unbelief-faith quest, are here firmly closed.

(c) Considered indifference

In addition to the kind of indifference which can be described in terms of motivation along the lines of interest, and distinct from it, there is an indifference characterised by *considered activity*. Its limits are set by the consideration or reflection which produces it. This indifference applies to those activities which are expressed in the language of conscious discipline. It has to do with power methodically exercised.

We may recall at this level the reference to *technological mastery*, conceived of as an achievement of reason. Technology here goes beyond science by integrating practice into it. At its extreme it produces our present-day self-sufficient world, to which the name of 'technocracy' is given, and which leaves room for nothing outside itself, whether irrational or of a different kind of rationality, even when it has not itself achieved certainty.

In the *order of society*, commitment to developing a particular social structure often plays the same sort of motivating role, which entails indifference to 'everything else'. It is a question then either of *effective operational structures*, or of reference to an *ideology* which expresses the rationality of a collective coherence appropriate to man.

Finally, the idea of a *Utopia* may express religious indifference by its rejection of everything beyond its imaginary horizon, which is closely linked to an actual social project.

There is a curious intermingling these days of precisely defined plans, such as we have been discussing, and convictions which arouse a religious concern, though indifference remains the essential feature of the experience. Active people who are convinced of the priority of Marxist scientific materialism may recognise that the products of religious culture are not to be despised. Sometimes this partially opens the way to a new debate. It can happen, for example, that a person totally committed to a particular ideology may learn to respect unreservedly some person with Christian faith, or some other conviction, and consult him with confidence about the rightness of a course of action.

But, overall, a widespread religious indifference has been built up today on power which repudiates any reference to the sacred.

(d) Indifference as an experience of emptiness and absence

On the heels of indifference related to localised knowledge and power of action comes what seems in some ways to be its very opposite—namely, the 'so what?' (already referred to) of certain groups of young people, or the total resignation of certain sections of the elderly. These constitute another kind of indifference, in which it is accepted that life is a basic absence of any hope of a better kind of existence. Human life is in itself simply emptiness.

In this case no kind of symbolism remains, for there is no longer any possible relation between action and an existence to direct. For some people, resignation to the present moment is enough; such resignation has the appearance of sovereign, timeless wisdom. For others, the aesthetic experience of the beauty of a sonata at a given moment is combined with the sense of perishability and nothingness which will follow. For others, again, the nihilism of the 'eternal return' is enough.

In fact for many of our contemporaries the impossible dream of mastery over death and suffering produces a latent despair for which there is no remedy. Does not our very technological efficiency put us in a position where we feel we have to give up the struggle, by placing before us the possibility, much more extreme than the scandal of the death of the individual, of using nuclear power to destroy humanity? And in the moral sphere who can shed light on the dark mystery of the suffering and sacrifice of children and the mentally handicapped?

In this context two possible attitudes of religious indifference emerge: either cultural stoicism, or a fatalism which closes its eyes to the death and evil which may exist beyond the distractions of action. Can this be said to be disinterest in its definitive form, or is there perhaps a chance that it may be disinterestedness?

(e) The indifference of decision—or anti-relation

It must be added that the religious indifference which is reached by way of the experience of emptiness and absence is more acute when it finds expression in a decision than when it is simply an involuntary, un-thought-out, giving up. And the acceptance of indifference to any hope of living in a sensible way plumbs the greatest depths when it involves the decision that every human partner is insignificant.

The person who is indifferent then refuses to express his non-sense, because he lacks any existing real person, capable of recognising his experience (even if it be an experience of nothingness), with whom to enter into dialogue. Gone then is the most elementary solidarity with comrades, gone the possibility (which may exist for the person most lacking in certainty) of finding life in the compassion or forgiveness which 'someone' may offer him. The disillusioned 'terrorist', who had chosen this role to escape from himself, would be our ultimate model of religious indifference. Niet. Nichts. Not just nothing, but—no one!

We mentioned positive disinterest, and disinterestedness. Is the adventure at an end? Can the question still be asked: how can one go on living with it? If time is part of the structure of human existence, the decision about indifference must take account of it. The world goes on, and changes, and the unforeseeable undertow of this heavy tide beats on the shores of our personal qualities of endurance and modifies them. By this unforeseeable development happening in the course of time, our indifferences are subjected to chances and risks which may increase or shatter our disinterest.

(f) The indifference of youth, or the risk of change

There is one situation of indifference which takes precedence over the others: that of youth. We have referred to it in connection with the extreme situation of the unthinking 'so what?'. In this respect and in practice the younger generations sometimes go farthest in their religious indifference. But youth is the human group with the longest future ahead of it. For this reason it is subject to possible change, either because of itself, or because of future events. This is why the indifference of young people runs the risk of change and sometimes of swinging over to its opposite. For example, awareness of death as a dimension of life can become strong enough to make young men and women swing over from indifference to the blind faith of a religious society or of a sect, quite unconditionally. This *indifference* with its *risk of change* makes impossible any kind of dialogue in face of the real and unforeseeable future.[3]

4. RELIGIOUS INDIFFERENCE AS A CHALLENGE AND A SIGN OF HOPE

We are therefore presented, today, with a certain 'geography' of religious indifference. This is, of course, the exploration of only one area among very many others. There are a great number of nuances within each of our provisional categories. The articles in this issue of *Concilium* will spell out their inadequacies or possible relevance. In conclusion I would like simply to draw attention to the *challenge* and the *opportunity* presented by this universe of indifference, since there is no question of being able to live without it.

We may perhaps indicate, then, two opportunities which this challenge offers. The first is that it reveals the wide scope of salvation even where the word itself is not used. For people exist who, by their very existence, hoping or despairing without saying so, raise the question of the meaning of human life by the way they live and by the very vastness of their numbers, and take it beyond the researches of either the believer or the agnostic. They are, as Balthasar said, witnesses to the Father's creation, prior to any utterance of the Word Incarnate. Thereby, and this is the second consequence of religious indifference, we, both believers and agnostics, are faced with the mystery of the Call addressed to us by a sacred history which cannot ignore the relation of all those people to the ultimate goal of humanity—even if that relation is negative.

Thus religious indifference is an invitation to us to welcome a new historical phenomenon, involving an infinity of human existences, and to recognise that we can only worship through the experience of our relations with each one of them, including those who forget us.

Translated by G. W. S. Knowles

Notes

1. We might have pursued the study of those currents of ideas which present themselves as *new expressions of doctrinal atheism*. This is not, however, the object of the present study, since the issue there is not religious indifference but considered opposition to 'the God hypothesis'. On the basis of various studies we can identify the following currents:—

(*a*) Neo-atheism taken up by L. Sève in a recasting of Marxism. Christianity has its place in relation to Marxism, but it remains no more than a witness to the imaginary which has never been eliminated.

(*b*) A form of neo-atheism is to be seen in the struggle of the *polytheism* of the new right against reductive monotheism. The gods are the source of equality and fraternity. See M. Debenoît and his writings.

(*c*) P. H. Levy: We are the ones who are; God is the one who does not exist.

(*d*) Michael Serres: The 'cosmic and intelligible flow of the world' envelops us and determines what we are.

2. With regard to the concept of 'attitude', there is no more adequate explanation than that given by Eric Weil in *Logique de la Philosophie* (Paris) pp. 70-72, and, in particular, this passage: 'How can man express in speech what he experiences in his history? By defining the *categories* of his *attitudes*. *Attitude* means the way in which a man conducts himself in the world. Normally this is unconscious; but it is always possible for speech to grasp it, to become conscious of it, by discerning the *essence* of it.'

3. *Sur la jeunesse*. An admirable analysis of youth as an example of indifference in the sense of the 'so what?' is presented by Shusaku Endo's novel *Un admirable idiot* (Paris).

Robert Kress

Religious Indifference— Definition and Criteria

THE PROBLEM of this investigation is doubly difficult. The first difficulty is the very definition of religion. The second is the nature and number of criteria by which religious practice can be judged. A brief discussion of these two difficulties will be followed by reflections on the practice of religion in the United States of America.

1. DEFINITION OF RELIGION

Not infrequently both proponents and opponents of religion are pleased to define religion extremely narrowly, thus restricting it to very limited and often marginal populations. This is advantageous for opponents, for it clearly marginalises religion as a human phenomenon. It is advantageous for some proponents, for it equates religion with their particular religion, thus 'guaranteeing' the veracity and obligatory nature of that particular religion, while others in general are accused of defining religion so widely and loosely that the term is completely void of identifiable content. In both cases it is clear that the definition of religion determines the criteria of both religions and interest and religious indifference.

How is religion to be defined? The Latin etymological approach is insufficient, because it is not clear in itself and is, in any case, restricted to Latin and its derivative languages. The dialectical approach, which can be traced back to S. Kierkegaard, which peaked systematically in K. Barth and which has been variously operative in theologians such as E. Brunner, H. Thielicke, E. Ebeling and D. Bonhoeffer, for whom a supposedly 'religionless world' would provide a sterling opportunity for the Christian faith, has been seen to be too narrow and one-sided, not adequately corresponding to observable human phenomena.[1] The approach of P. Ricoeur, which would require the death of religion in order that true faith might flower, suffers from the same deficiencies.[2] It is also not legitimate to restrict religion to only those phenomena which would be entirely without spot or wrinkle (Eph. 5:27), for religion, as at least and also human, can have not only a positive nature and essence (*Wesen*), but also a deformed one (*Unwesen*).[3] Furthermore, traditional religions (for example, certain forms of Buddhism) have been atheistic, not requiring a personal God. Even among the religions which are theistic, the deity is so diversely conceived that a common understanding of either god or the relationship of the non-godly to the god can hardly be achieved.

Against this background recourse can legitimately be made to the phenomenological or anthropological definition of religion.[4] This approach abstracts from all the problems above as well as all direct considerations of right or wrong, true or false, good or evil. It approaches religion as observable human behaviour and describes it as the efforts of humanity, individual and corporate, to deal with finitude, the totality of human life and experience, the meaning of life, ultimate concern. As such, religion is the attempt of human beings to discern the dictates of conscience and to live accordingly. In this wide sense I prefer to define religion as the organisation of human life/being, individually and socially, on the basis of insights (the true) and values (the good) perceived to be ultimate.

Admittedly, on this basis all human beings and societies are religious. Although this may seem to be begging the question, it is not. It only records general patterns of behaviour which can be observed among human beings, whatever their particular articulations. As such, it neither offers nor applies criteria of truth, goodness, beauty. It allows for what P. Tillich describes as 'quasi-religions', modern (secular) movements whose members are in a 'state of being grasped by an ultimate concern, a concern which qualifies all other concerns as preliminary and which itself contains the answer to the question of the meaning of life'.[5] Furthermore, this approach to religion also corresponds to the nature of human being as this has been revealed by the classic critique of religion (L. Feuerbach, K. Marx, S. Freud, F. Nietzsche). Their critique does not expose human nature as a-religious. It does expose traditional religions as false, bad and inhuman. However, the salvation these inadequate past religions of God were supposed to have provided for human need will be supplied by the new religion of man, in which man is both God and saviour unto man.[6] Again, this is not begging the question in favour of traditional religions or a particular religion. As R. Panikkar notes, 'The aim of any religion is to save or free Man. No matter how we interpret this salvation or liberation, religion is always the means whereby Man arrives at his destination. . . .'[7] This desire for salvation is so *humanly* religious that it is present not only in the traditional theistic and non-theistic religions, but also clearly in secular versions like Marxism,[8] not only in theory but also in 'Eastern countries [which] feature a number of religious and pseudo-religious movements'.[9] I emphasise 'humanly religious', for all religion is rooted in human beings' 'fundamental need for meaningful fulfilment beyond the mere satisfaction of material needs . . . they look to ends which transcend individual existence'.[10] A similar general understanding of religion as a human phenomenon, restricted to neither traditional theistic nor modern non-theistic forms, is clearly evidenced by various decisions of United States Courts.[11] According to the Supreme Court, secular humanism is properly regarded as a religion; it is also possible to believe in god, where the 'g' is lower case. The Ninth Circuit Court of Appeals regarded as a religious belief 'man thinking his highest, feeling his deepest and living his best'. It also accepted human belief in the 'goodness' or even the 'livingness' in the very heart of things as religious. Thus, religion properly describes 'a given belief that is sincere and meaningful [and which] occupies a place in the life of the possessor paralleled to that filled by orthodox belief in God' (*Seeger*). What this approach does is to indicate 'equivalents' for the traditional deity in religions. In my own definition above, the role of the deity in traditional theistic religions is expanded to the notion of ultimate insights and values; A. N. Whitehead speaks of 'what is permanent in the nature of things'.[12] Although not everyone may perceive the ultimate and the permanent similarly, all do perceive some ultimate something/one permanent. And they live accordingly. Hence, as such, no one can be without religion, and there can be no religious indifference.

The point of all this is, of course, to emphasise that an inquiry about a possible increase in religious indifference can be properly made only within the context of any given, particular religion in concrete circumstances. The question is never, as L. Korinek points out in regard to Nietzsche, whether human beings are religious—only whether they belong to and practise this or that religion.[13]

2. CRITERIA

Since human being is necessarily religious in at least a wide sense, the discussion of religious interest or indifference can take place only within any given single religion. However, even this is a difficult task, for the criteria whereby such interest or indifference is to be discerned are not immediately clear and distinct. One can read the entire Judaeo-Christian tradition as a debate about the criteria of the true worshipper of God (John 4:23) the true son of Abraham (Matt. 3:9), the true Jew (Rom. 2:27-29).

The difficulty of discerning interest or indifference is compounded because religion consists of both an inner attitude and outer actions, which are to express this attitude in the intersubjective relationships of human time and space. In general, the absence of outer good works calls into question the very existence of inner faith (James 2:14-23). As the fruit reveals the tree (Matt. 7:15-20; 12:33-37), so do the disciples' actions reveal their discipleship (Matt. 7:21-23). True religion demands the correspondence between inner attitude and both ethical conduct and ritual celebration (Matt. 5:23-26).

Because of the difficulty of reading the hearts and minds of human beings, we are impelled to establish outer works as the criteria of religious interest/indifference. So, the critical question is the kind and number of outer religious works required to indicate the presence of religious interest or indifference.[14] Christianity faced a crisis when the age of martyrs passed. What was the new criterion of religious interest and commitment to be? Symbolically, the monk replaced the martyr. Gradually, in Roman Catholicism the monachised, celibate, ordained priest became the model and criterion of religious commitment, there being some dispute between secular and religious priests about ultimate preference.[15] Generally, studies of religious commitment have focused on this class of religionists. The outer actions most frequently performed by them became the generally, if implicitly, accepted criteria for the religious interest of not only all Catholics, but all human beings.

This narrow focus was not counterbalanced by the classic triad of prayer, fasting and almsgiving. This triad itself, although available to all, was in fact understood in terms of the forms (*Gestalt*) it took in the dominant clerical subculture. Not only does this approach focus on outer works as the criteria of religiosity, it also focuses on a highly restricted set of such works. Unfortunately, this congeries of works is such that to be religious seems *ipso facto* to be unworldly. The natural consequence of this process is to define most humans as unreligious. However, as K. Rahner has noted in regard to the relationship of theism and atheism, the battle against such unreligiousness may be most importantly a battle against the inadequacy of our own understanding of religions.[16] The primary problem may not be the sin and indifference of the others, but the narrowness of our own understanding.

In any consideration of religious interest or indifference, we do well to recall the words of James (1:27): 'pure and unspoiled religion in the eyes of God this—coming to the help of widows and orphans and keeping oneself uncontaminated. . . .' And we should immediately note how general these criteria are, how open to various historical concretisations. Worthwhile, too, is Jesus' declaration that one can be 'virtuous' and 'blessed', one of the sheep, although one is not even reflectively aware of the criteria. A striking statement about the ambiguity of religious criteria, in its own way a confirmation of Jesus' understanding, is Vatican II's doctrine that even the atheist can satisfy the criteria required for salvation.[17]

Clearly, then, a mathematical decrease in the frequency of the customary concrete criteria of outer works does not necessarily entail an increase in religious indifference. Indeed, what seemed to be a decline may be a revelation that previous ages were not so religious after all[18]—and thus a purification of our ideas of both religion and criteria of religion.

3. RELIGION IN THE UNITED STATES

In contrast to some other Western nations, religion seems to be flourishing in the United States even today, and even according to the customary criteria such as church attendance, explicit belief in God and such like.[19] A recent study indicates that 95 per cent of Americans believe in God, 71 per cent in life after death, 84 in heaven, 67 in hell. In regard to the Ten Commandments, 93 per cent agreed that the prohibitions against murder and theft still applied, 87 per cent those against adultery. Whether they go or not, 81 per cent considered themselves religious; 48 per cent of all Americans said that God was most important in their lives. All these percentages are higher, often considerably, than those of Western European countries. Also noteworthy is the finding of another study that although two of every five Roman Catholics discontinue church practice, usually between the ages of sixteen and twenty-five, most do return to the Church and church practice later on.[20]

This has led some to speak of a peculiarly American 'civil religion'. However, as we shall see later, this concept is not very helpful. Much more to the point is R. Knox's still valid contention that 'The American continent has more than once been the scene of such an adventure [a sectarian theocracy on the frontier, in the wilderness]; in these days it is the last refuge of the enthusiast.'[21] Properly understood, this statement requires that enthusiasm be taken primarily not as *Schwärmerei*, but literally as 'in God', for enthusiasts understand themselves to possess and be possessed by God. There is such an enthusiastic religious dimension in the American consciousness.

What are the reasons for this state of affairs? Although religious protest and emancipation from national State churches were not the only reasons for the founding of the new nation, they were crucially important. The federal constitution was not intended to establish a wall of separation between Church and State, but to ensure the growth of true religion and to prevent the federal, national government from imposing one religion on the entire nation; individual states such as Massachusetts did have estabished churches. For the revolutionary generation a prime concern was the 'State's patronage of religion [in] the interest of fostering public morality'.[22] The contemporary argument about prayer in the public schools continues this concern. President R. Reagan often quotes George Washington's statement: 'Of all the dispositions which lend to political prosperity, religion and morality are indispensable supports.' On the National Day of Prayer, Reagan emphasised: 'How can we hope to retain our freedom through the generations if we fail to teach our young that our liberty springs from an abiding faith in our Creator. . . . I have never believed that (separation of Church and State) was supposed to protect us from religion. It was to protect religion from government tyranny.'[23] In this, he is true to the founding generation. As T. O. Hanley notes: 'They were content that they had disestablished a Church of England without disestablishing Christianity.'[24] In contrast to the French and Soviet, the American revolution is characterised by a positive relationship between the new nation and the old religion.

This positive relationship was possible because the United States as such never had an official national State church. Hence, it was spared the trauma of the oppressive *cuius regio eius religio*. This non-establishment was permanently established by the revolution and the Constitution. Thus, S. Lipset explains that 'the United States is the only Protestant country. By "Protestant" I am referring to Protestant sects as opposed to State churches. . . . The majority of Americans . . . from practically the beginning of the Republic down to the present have been members of churches that are not supported by the State and, in turn, do not support the State.'[25] The sectarian and radical Protestant church experience (Anabaptist, Puritans, Pietists) not only provided for a new relationship between religion (not Church!) and State, but also found in America not only the New World, but the new Israel, new Eden, new Promised Land. In this 'Wilderness Zion' (John Winthrop) true Christianity (in contrast to the fallen Christianity of the established churches in Europe) would give birth to the true kingdom of God. This primitivist enthusiasm no longer perdures as such; in fact, these original radical churches can be perceived to have become today's establishment.[26] Nevertheless, the 'life, liberty and pursuit of happiness' optimism and energy which it originally inspired persists in contemporary America, not only in the words of the Declaration of Independence, but in the aspirations of the American people. Ample evidence is provided by the survey cited above: 80 per cent of Americans said that they were very proud to be citizens of their country; in case of war, 71 per cent would fight for their country; 84 per cent take a great deal of pride in their work. Answers to the same questions from Japanese and Western Europeans ranged from 21 to 66 per cent.[27]

Of all the statistics in this survey, the most important concerns freedom: 72 per cent of Americans chose personal freedom over equality, which was chosen by only 20 per cent. Equality was described thus: 'nobody is underprivileged and social class differences are not so strong.' In England 69 per cent choose freedom, in Europe overall 49. This emphasis on freedom is confirmed by a Canadian living in Europe and reacting to the 'growing climate of anti-Americanism' he perceives there. He emphasises 'that splendid confusion (read, if you like, "liberty") that makes you the great people you really are'. He also notes the spontaneity, ability and willingness to change as well as the variety of the American population.[28] Similar observations are made by two German commentators. One emphasises that 'in America nothing is univocal' (*Nichts ist in Amerika eindeutig*) in connection with America's faith in the goodness of man and its striving for personal fulfilment and satisfaction.[29] The other develops the contrast between Europe, which chose, from the French revolution's triad, equality, and America, which chose freedom, its preservation at home and promotion abroad. He also notes the continuity of this emphasis on freedom throughout the entire history of the nation—even today when American policies are often judged oppressive.[30] I recount these evaluations not to claim that American actions have always been purely disinterested (but, then, whose have?) or always correct, but only to highlight its unflagging enthusiasm for freedom. From the revolutionary Patrick Henry's 'Give me liberty or give me death' to the motto on the automobile licences of contemporary Vermont, 'Live free or die', freedom always takes precedence.

I thus emphasise freedom because the American interest in religion cannot be appreciated apart from it. Two points must be understood. First, governmental policy must arrange for the maximum freedom of the citizenry, including freedom of religion. This preoccupation with freedom affects all attempts at legislation, whether in regard to racism, drunk driving, abortion, identity cards for citizens or immigrant labourers, mandatory helmets for motor-cycle riders—from the most trivial to the most serious. This preoccupation with freedom can be an obstacle in the reform of unjust social conditions. However, on the part of both privileged and underprivileged, liberal and conservative, freedom remains the clarion call—often with the reminder that our forefathers fought and died precisely for this constitutionally guaranteed freedom.

Of course, this preoccupation with freedom does not guarantee that all share equally in its benefits. In fact, minorities such as Roman Catholics and Blacks have not.[31] On the other hand, the non-establishment, voluntary nature of both civil and religious society in America gives all an opportunity to shape both their own identities as well as that of the nation at large. Furthermore, in a pluralist society a healthy competition can develop among the churches (religions) so that all are challenged to function more effectively. This has in fact been the case among the (various) Protestant and Catholic churches in the past, and among an even greater variety today.[32] Without doubt, a chief reason for the flourishing of religion in America today is the freedom that both the Constitution and history, both civil and religious, have provided.

This brings us to the second point, a corollary of the first: the preoccupation with freedom requires (not only allows, as in the first point) that religion flourish. This is the point of the earlier quotations from Presidents Washington and Reagan—without the moral foundation traditionally provided by religion, the freedom so desired cannot be sustained. This is the argument invoked in favour of voluntary prayer in the public schools, currently unconstitutional. It is also the reason for the current proliferation of private, Christian (often called Bible schools!) schools especially by Protestants, who could formerly rely on the public schools to provide, although unofficially, a Christian education. Clearly, many of these schools have also been inspired by a racist flight from integrated public schools. But it is also clear that a more compelling reason has been the flight from 'valueless' secular humanist education and the desire for a religious, Christian education—which will provide a secure foundation for the freedom which will otherwise, it is feared, be lost.[33] It is not naive to understand that it is this preoccupation with the preservation of freedom which prompts the desire for observable religious elements in public life and institutions. It need not be racism, anti-Semitism, anti-Catholicism, sexism, classism, as some superficial observers contend.[34] Incarceration and even capital punishment need not be inspired by pharisaic self-righteousness. Free citizens spontaneously understand that their freedom is endangered by ever more restrictive and comprehensive legal and other restraints if violations of freedom and order are not contained. And soon no one will be free. It is the insurance of this freedom that prompts public advocacy and nurture of religion—not imposition of a State church—in the United States.

The distinctive hallmark of religion in the United States, and the precise reason why there is no religious indifference, is the positive mutual correlationship of religion and freedom, in the written Constitution as well as the lived society, past and present.

4. REFLECTIONS

'Civil religion', the term R. Bellah adapted from Rousseau's *Social Contract*, IV, 8, does not adequately describe the American religious phenomenon.[35] It is a polyvalent term. At least five definitions are recounted by R. Rickley and D. Jones.[36] M. A. Neal is probably correct when she says that Bellah 'speaks more as priest than sociologist', although he intends his work to be sociological.[37] This view is supported by Bellah's emphasis on the role of civil religion as the judge of the nation's success in subordinating itself to ethical principles. This may coincide with Bellah's own religious convictions and tradition, but it does not describe the positive messianic aspirations of the non-conformist, radical, sectarian religionists who gave the United States its particular and peculiar religious orientation. He is, consequently, not on target when he posits civil religion as the 'national faith', a third alternative to Christianity and the 'American Way of Life'.[38] The national faith, if one wishes to speak thus, is (has been, at least) a unique way of being Christian, voluntary and non-conformist, and of bringing this Christianity to bear on public life, whether one was non-conformist or confessional Protestant or Catholic.

Of monumental importance for the current survival and flourishing of religion in America has been its pluralist experience from the very beginning. Minority religions certainly, and even dominant religions (churches), have always had to deal with other possibilities of religious allegiance. Hence, adherence to any church has always been a matter of choice. In so choosing, one could achieve a partial consent, identification and adherence, having explicitly or implicitly adopted elements from the other religious options available.[39] This variety again allowed for a freedom of religion not always available in other nations.

Since, unfortunately, this variety of churches and religions did not always live together peacefully, those churches which were the object of nativist and other bigotries had to intensify their commitment in order to survive and flourish. Likewise, although religion can be an analgesic for oppressed people, the Black American experience clearly demonstrates that religion can also be a strengthening and liberating agency. 'Negro Spirituals', as they have been called, are stirring witness to religion's ability to encourage resistance to oppression and striving for liberation—again, freedom. Against the standard tenets of the traditional critique of religion,[40] the American experience, at least so far, has shown that religion does not require the alienation of bad socio-economic conditions or sexual repression, that freedom and prosperity do not require religious indifference.[41]

5. CONCLUSION

An observation of J. Maritain is apt to help us understand the current contrast of the American experience of religion, in general and in particular: 'There is indeed one thing that Europe knows well and knows only too well; that is the tragic significance of life. . . . There is one thing that America knows well . . .: it is the value and dignity of the common man, the value and dignity of the people . . . that the common man has a right to the "pursuit of happiness"; the pursuit of the elementary conditions and possessions which are the prerequisites of a free life. . . .'[42]

This difference between the tragic sense and the pursuit of happiness I would attribute not only to geography and history in general, but to the original and continuing American religious experience, which essentially excludes religious indifference.

Notes

1. As even the *Taschenlexikon Religion und Theologie*, 3rd ed. E. Fahlbusch (Göttingen 1971) p. 261.

2. P. Ricouer *The Conflict of Interpretations* (Evanston 1974) p. 441.

3. E. Welte 'Wesen und Unwesen der Religion' *Auf der Spur des Ewigen* (Freiburg 1965) pp. 279-296.

4. See W. Riess *Glaube als Konsens* (Munich 1979) pp. 173-178.

5. P. Tillich *Christianity and the Encounter of the World Religions* (New York 1961) p. 4.

6. See B. Casper *Wesen und Grenzen der Religionskritik* (Würzburg 1974).

7. R. Panikkar *Myth, Faith and Hermeneutics* (New York 1979) p. 408.

8. L. Dupre *The Other Dimension* (New York 1979).

9. I. Fetscher 'State Socialist Ideology as Religion' *Christianity and Socialism* ed. J. B. Metz and J. P. Jossua, *Concilium* (105) 82. See also *Häresien der Zeit* ed. A. Böhm (Freiburg 1961) esp. pp. 215-374.

10. *Ibid*, Fetscher, p. 85.

11. The cases are: *Torcaso* v. *Watkins*, 397 US 488 (1961) at 495, n. 11; *United States* v. *Seeger*, 380 US 193 (1965); *Peter* v. *United States*, 324 F. 2d 173 (9th Cir. 1963); *Macmurray* v. *United States*, 330 F. 2d 928 (9th Cir. 1964).

12. A. N. Whitehead *Religion in the Making* (New York 1960) p. 16.

13. L. Korinek 'Psicologia della nagazione di Dio' in *Psicologia dell' atheismo* (Rome 1967) pp. 42, 74.

14. See, for example, the studies of J. Fitcher, J. Thomas in the United States and of G. Schmidtchen in Germany.

15. See R. Kress *The Church: Communion, Sacrament and Communication* (Washington 1982) ch. 4.

16. K. Rahner 'Kirche und Atheismus' *Strimmen der Zeit*, 106 (1981) 12.

17. *Lumen Gentium*, § 16; *Gaudium et Spes*, §§ 19-22; *Ad Gentes*, § 7. See K. Rahner 'Atheismus und implizites Christentum' *Schriften zur Theologie* 8 (Einsiedeln 1967) pp. 187-212.

18. See J. Delumeau *Le Catholicisme entre Luther et Voltaire* (Paris 1971).

19. These data are from a study conducted by the Center for Applied Research in the Apostolate, Washington, DC, in conjunction with the Gallup organisation. The results will be published in book form in the future. The data here are taken from the NC new release as reported in *The Catholic Register* (Canada, 4 June 1982) 7.

20. D. R. Hoge *Converts, Dropouts and Returnees* (Washington 1982).

21. R. Knox *Enthusiasm* (Oxford 1950) p. 3; see also pp. 578, 585.

22. T. O. Hanley 'Church/State Relations in the American Revolutionary Era' in *America in Theological Perspective* ed. T. McFadden (New York 1976) p. 90.

23. R. Reagan 'Address to the K of C' *Origins* 12 (1982) 172. The second quotation is related by J. Lackey 'Reagan Endorses School Prayer Amendment' *The Message* (Evansville, Ind., 14 May 1982) 2.

24. Hanley, in the article cited in note 22, p. 91.

25. S. Lipset 'Religion in American Politics' in *Capitalism and Socialism* ed. M. Novak (Washington 1979) p. 61.

26. See F. H. Littell 'The Radical Reformation and the American Experience' in McFadden, the work cited in note 22, pp. 81-85.

27. In footnote 19.

28. D. J. Hall 'America: Living Up to the Image' *The Christian Century* 99 (19 May 1982) 589

29. H. von Borch *Amerika—Dekadenz und Grösse* (Munich 1981).

30. H. C. Schröder *Die Amerikanische Revolution* (Munich 1982).

31. See J. Hennessey *American Catholics* (New York 1981); *The Black Experience in Religion* ed. C. Eric Lincoln (New York 1974).

32. See J. Saliba 'The Christian Church and the New Religious Movements: Towards Theological Understanding' *Theological Studies* 43 (1982) 468-485.

33. See R. Gibbons 'Textbooks in the Hollows' *Commonweal* (6 December 1971) 221-234; J. Elshtain 'Time to Politicize the Schools' *The Nation* (25 September 1982) 257, 267-271.

34. As does the entirely unfortunate book of D. C. Maguire *The New Subversives* (New York 1982), whose admittedly precipitate preparation (see the 'Acknowledgments') cannot serve as an excuse. Although the book does succeed in pointing out some of the deficiencies of the 'Religious Right', it succeeds equally in demonstrating the same deficiencies and self-righteous intolerance on the part of the 'Liberal', whether secular or religious. What clearly alarms Maguire and other liberal ideologues like him is precisely 'the power they [the New Right] are amassing' (p. 3), for this implies that the liberal, secular humanist establishment, which has been the growing and greater power in American government, society, and life of late, is losing some of its power. Only the naive or like minded ideological adepts would argue that liberals of the left are more tolerant than conservatives of the right. The correct appreciation is that both are tolerant and intolerant about different objects.

35. On Civil Religion, the handiest compact sources are M. A. Neal 'Civil Religion, Theology,

and Politics in America' and M. L. Schneider 'A Catholic Perspective on American Civil Religion' in McFadden *America In Theological Perspective* pp. 99-122, 123-139.

36. *American Civil Religion* eds. R. Rickey and D. Jones (New York 1974).

37. M. A. Neal, in McFadden, cited in note 22, p. 102.

38. R. Bellah 'Civil Religion in America' *Daedalus* 96 (1967) 1-21.

39. On the importance and problem, theological, of partial, minimal and maximal consent, adherence and identification of members with a church or religion, see Riess, the work cited in note 4, at pp. 81-261.

40. So, although the 'Kritik der Religion' may be the 'Voraussetzung aller Kritik', as Karl Marx (*Die Frühschriften* (Stuttgart 1953) p. 341) urged, the American experience of religion requires a different critique than heretofore offered.

41. One of the most interesting efforts on the contemporary American religious scene is Michael Novak's attempt to develop theologically the positive correlationship between democratic capitalism and the Judaeo-Christian religious tradition. See his *Toward a Theology of the Corporation* (Washington 1981) and *The Spirit of Democratic Capitalism* (New York 1982).

42. J. Maritain *Reflections on America* (New York 1958) pp. 194-195.

Joseph Spae

Religious Indifference—
The Japanese Way

WHEN THE editors asked me to write on 'religious indifference found in a civilisation other than Christian, Japan for example', they presented me and their readers with a considerable challenge. Indeed, my framework will be different from that of the other contributors. Religion, in Japan, does not quite mean what it means in the West; nor does 'religious indifference' cover the Western range of ideas. To everything Japanese there is a touch and a tonality not readily grasped by people unacquainted with Japanese culture.

To put this in a nutshell: Our discussion must take into account the fact that religion, in Japan, is as much, if not more, an affair of the nation and the family than of the individual. Religious belonging is often multiple: the average Japanese, statistically speaking, has 1·7 religions. Both religious belonging and its expression are often seasonal. They respond to the life-cycle: Shinto at birth, Christianity or any other personal religion in adult life, Buddhism in the third age, and a bit of all at death. Most Japanese feel that religion is an affair of the heart, and not of the head. It is accepted and practised for reasons of affection towards somebody, say, your ancestors and your friends, rather than for reasons of conviction. Religion is seen more as an ethic than a dogmatic. It is a loving intuition with a mystical and aesthetic allure and not submission to a logical chain of arguments. We have a standard saying in Japan: 'In catechetics, win an argument and lose a soul.' Schematically presented, and with the necessary caveats about all sorts of marginality, East and West could be compared in the antithetic categories shown in the chart opposite.
Obviously, religious indifference is the opposite side of the coin; and it is equally impervious to an accurate definition. It is true that, in Japan as in the West, religious indifference is abetted by the moral climate of society, by an eventual discredit of the churches and temples, by a nonchalance about ultimate concerns, the popular critique of official and private religious behaviour, and even by a syncretistic mind resulting from a better understanding of the unity and diversity of all religions and of the parallelism of the ways of salvation which they hold out. It is also true in East and West that many well-meaning people recognise the possibility of an authentic, even spiritual and mystical human life without the need for any specific religious belonging. More boldly sated: a religious belonging is easily seen by many Japanese as a potential obstacle to that peace and joy which are the birthright of a person fully alive.

20

RELIGION AND RELIGIOUS INDIFFERENCE, JAPANESE AND WESTERN		
Characteristics	Japanese	Western
Quality	intuitive	reflective
Tonality	emotional	volitional
Multiplicity	inclusive	exclusive
Finality	this-worldly	other-worldly
Range	communal	individual
Belonging	diffused	institutional
Content	ethical	dogmatic

I shall say no more about the specificity of Japanese religiosity (a word which, for obvious reasons, I prefer to 'religion') beyond inviting the reader to have a look at a full treatment of the matter in my *Japanese Religiosity* (Tokyo: Oriens Institute, 1971).

1. FOUR FACETS OF JAPANESE RELIGIOUS LIFE

The generalities I have mentioned could be conveniently packaged in the four paragraphs which follows:

(*a*) Japan's *inclination to the impersonal* in matters of religion is at the origin of her non-personal description of God. Japan's Shinto-inspired optimism and inner-worldliness does not conceive of God as totally different from man. The Buddhist current of her spirituality, which is, in this case, less influential than that of Shinto, does not find God in this world, but in the nirvana of the next. Understandably then, Japan's theism tends towards identification and participation; it is panentheism. The gods are always near and benevolent. Man does not feel lonesome nor abandoned. From this unthematic and prereflexive approach to the divine, the Japanese have developed their emotionally rich theomorphism, a stance which has all the earmarks of an outspoken homo-cosmo-centrism.

(*b*) The *god-man closed circle* which is basic to Shinto is responsible for the particular soteriological aspects of Japanese religious thought. Salvation, in the broad sense, has, throughout Japan's history, always been connected with the various forms of filial piety: towards living parents, it is *kōkō*, the traditional and most powerful incentive for social conformity. Towards the corporate personality of the nation, embodied in the emperor institution (rather than in the emperor as person), it takes the name of *chū*, loyalty. In either case, familial or national, Japanese soteriology had the effect of what Joseph M. Kitagawa, in his *Religion in Japanese History* (New York, Columbia University Press, 1966) has called 'an immanental theocracy'. In either case, too, an agency of authority and order became sacralised, and the response to its beneficial guidance took the form of a virtue with deep religious overtones.

How this virtue will survive the recent social changes remains to be seen. A transfer of loyalties is not ruled out. Such a transfer (and I believe that it is already taking place) would put the individual more at the centre of his own salvation. That salvation is seen more and more as man's yearning for a greater share in spiritual and material benefits, this time no longer obtained through parental and governmental favours, but rather through one's personal decision and toil. Such a desacralisation of the salvation idea is inevitable in modern Japanese society. But, looked at from a Christian point of view, it could be welcomed as a hidden door which opens upon man's insufficiency when he must confront the ultimate issues of life. Thence a new vista of hope might unfold as he discovers for himself the way by which 'the universe itself is to be freed from the shackles of mortality and enter upon the liberty and splendour of the children of God' (Rom. 8:21).

(c) In present-day Japanese religiosity, *'salvation' is expressed in a variety of ways*. A Shinto scholar writes: 'When man is separated from the *kami* or gods, the tragedy of this world begins.' For Zen, 'Man is a Buddha from the beginning . . .'. Shin Buddhism teaches that 'Salvation is instantly completed in the present through our faith. On acquiring faith, we are enveloped in eternal life.'

The newer religions are even more outspoken, perhaps in part under Christian influences. For Tenrikyō, the human body is a thing lent and ruled by God, the Parent. Death is called *denaoshi*, literally, 'to start afresh' which means to return the body to God in order to be reborn anew in this world. The formulation nearest to that of Christianity belongs to World Messianity: 'God's power and our wisdom are necessary for us to be saved from unhappiness. Our wisdom corresponds to truth, goodness and beauty. Life after death is the spiritual world of the divine nature. In this life, the harmonisation of spirit and body or divine nature and physical nature is the state of salvation.'

(d) These various expressions are *deeply ingrained in the Japanese soul*. In fact, they veil man's universal search for God. They are the unexpected but magnificent echoes of another type of language, that of the Bible: 'I stayed in your presence, you held my right hand. . . . I look to no one else in heaven, I delight in nothing else on earth' (Psalm 73:24-26). And it is because of this fact that the religions of Japan, notwithstanding essential differences with Christianity, are proof of 'a certain perception ᴏf that hidden power which hovers over the course of things and over the events of human life . . . and which instils the lives of her people with a profound religious sense' (Vatican II, Declaration of the Relationship of the Church to Non-Christian Religions, § 2).

I submit that a Japanese who distances himself from these four points, sociologically and religiously speaking, marginalises himself within his own society. He then becomes a person standing at the bifurcation of his spiritual journey. Either he turns into a no-religion individual, i.e., a person 'indifferent' to 'religion' and/or to any religious group; or he finds himself at a moment of life at which he obtains an untrammelled view of new religious possibilities. Official Japanese religious statistics emphatically show that few Japanese ever turn away from the traditional religiosity of their national past. In fact, most Japanese would feel offended if they were told that they are 'materialistic and irreligious', traits which they refuse to recognise in themselves. But, to the contrary most Japanese will agree that, for the sake of true religion, they have no 'religion', by which they intend to convey the idea that for the nonce they keep their decision in abeyance until they meet with a 'religion' worthy of their choice.

It is common observation in Japan that only a person who has reached 'a neutral point', feels free to make a personal religious choice. If anyone should call this neutral point 'religious indifference', I shall demur. In Japan, it is often concern for true religion which, in the West, would pass for unconcern. As a friend told me when I asked about his religion: 'I have no religion, hence I am now ready to come and listen to yours.'

2. JAPANESE ETHICS AND RELIGIOUS INDIFFERENCE

Applying an inductive method, it will be useful to find out what happens to the moral life in a society of the type we have described. Anticipating my conclusion, I submit that

Japanese morality will dictate one's religious choice, and not vice versa. Morality will be the touchstone of the seriousness of that choice; without morality, any 'religion' loses meaning; a religion's morality being accepted, that religion's creed will make no difference to the believer. Let me explain, and look at the matter through Japanese eyes.

Japanese ethicists rarely analyse the nature of good and evil. To them, metaphysical insights are unappealing. Even in Buddhism comparative ethics is completely absent. In Japan, the moral ideal is perceived in its existential application and not in its theoretical background. Theory is valued only as the confirmation, and not as the source, of moral rectitude. Awareness of a sublime, natural and inviolable, moral order is weak. Neither in Shinto nor in Buddhism do we find a 'god' who judges the merits of the human act. On the contrary, Buddhism teaches that the moral act carries its retribution within itself. Hence, in Japan, moral judgment—and 'religious indifference'—is of an extreme situational and contextual nature. For all that, there is a general feeling, of Buddhist origin, that man's behaviour is influenced, to a large extent, by factors beyond his control, such as his past and environment.

The reader might feel that this outlook must, of necessity, come close to moral indifferentism. Hence, let me immediately correct myself and remind him of an ancient Japanese and Buddhist saying: 'Each day is a good day.' The Japanese see life as a gift and an opportunity. Their outlook on morality is strongly immanent as is the whole texture of their religious life. This is abundantly made clear even in the very word that translates our 'ethics', *rinri*, which, in Japanese, means 'the principles which govern human relations'. In such a way of life, prime attention goes to 'the art of living', with its traditional insistence on poise, charm and etiquette which, I am convinced, are not merely secular values, but also the subtle expression of charity and consideration for others. Indeed, in Japan, traditional politeness and courtesy are seen as the hallmark of moral excellence.

The Japanese people, in their moral judgments, object to that either/or dichotomy which is typical of Western thought. They prefer by far the more hazy, and perhaps also more charitable, both/and approach which refuses to human acts the preset categories of good or bad. A certain moral tolerance (or is it 'indifference'?), frowned upon by the juridical mind, is interpreted by many Japanese as having *ningenmi*, 'a human flavour', that empathy for man's foibles and fickleness which refuses to sit in judgment upon one's neighbour's conduct. The psychological effect of such an attitude, as well as its cause, is the acceptance of the Golden Mean as an element of perfection. Whatever does violence to the person or to the situation is thereby also immoral. The good is the feasible, the durable, the totally human. This way of life is expressed in a well-known saying: 'Rice-cakes are better than flowers, *Hana yori dango*', a saying which reminds us of the Latin *'primum vivere, deinde philosophare'*. For short, to live, and to live well, is much more than to theorise about life.

Japanese society appears often to the Western observer as a thoroughly secularised world. Officially, there is complete separation of Church and State. There is a marked abandoning of traditional religious allegiances, some implications of which I have already tried to indicate. Again, let me ask, does this mean 'religious indifference' or 'secularisation' in the Western sense? I think not. Instead, I submit that the secularisation of Japan, which obviously has nothing to do with a turning away *from Christianity*, may open the nation's mind to new, international and ethical concerns, which, in final analysis, may become the turning point at which Japan shifts from a particularist to a universalistic morality, and from the vertical, authoritarian type of ethics to a horizontal person-to-person type. If I be allowed to dream aloud, this might mean that the Japanese ethic of the future will become ever more intensively confronted with elements of Christian origin, and, aligned with its own genius, capable of

C

harmoniously integrating all these ingredients into a splendid whole, thoroughly Japanese and, step by step, thoroughly Christian. On this path to the future—and, unless I am mistaken, it is already with us—to borrow an image of Nishida, Japan's most famous philosopher who came so close to the Christian faith, 'Western intelligence will meet with Eastern love, the zenith of intelligence'. If and when this happens, we shall all better understand that, in Nishida's words with which he concludes his famous *A Study of Good* (tr. by V. H. Viglielmo, Tokyo: Ministry of Education, 1960, p. 189): 'We Japanese who do not know God but who only love him and believe in him are the ones most able to know God.'

3. IN CONCLUSION: 'JAPANESE' RELIGIOUS INDIFFERENCE MAKES THE DIFFERENCE

By Western, Christian standards, the Japanese approach to morality and religion may seem negative, and hence betray 'indifference'. Yet, this conclusion would be unfair as well as false. Japanese religiosity and morality try, first and foremost, to eliminate the conditions which obstruct man's moral progress. This process is described in a negative terminology which is the Oriental way of indicating something positive. Then, too, the Japanese say, there is a legitimate *via negativa*, also in moral matters. What they negate is, in matters of religion, a lethargic way of life which refuses to strive for moral excellence. What they affirm here is the profound truth that man is in need of a *self-revolution* if he is ever to reach that *self-evolution* which his true self craves. Here is a laudable effort to eliminate 'dis-values', so that real values may be found. It is true, of course, that in Japan's traditional perspective, man's goal can be reached without the help of a saviour. This is a fact with which 'Western' thinking must come to grips as it opens its heart to the many-splendoured raiment in which God's loving-kindness manifests itself to this nation.

I know that on this difficult theme opinions differ, and that more research is needed, particularly by Japanese scholars themselves. In this matter, the theologian and the sociologist could work in collaboration and take an inventory of the religious happenings within their nation. The sociologist would examine the morality of an action and of a situation, trying to ascertain whether it agrees with man's nature and environment. The theologian would go one step further: he will study the religious quality of this influence in the light of the data of his faith and of that supreme exemplar of human perfection which is Christ. In assigning a quota of 'religious indifference' to Japan, sociologist and theologian will delight in the discovery of any movement towards interiorisation, any search for a *supplément d'âme*, the more human. It is precisely at this point that they will locate, in the plurality of moral options open to the Japanese and their society, the true nature of their religiosity. The first achievement of this search, and hence, of the quality of religious indifference in Japan, may well point to the 'birth of a new humanism in which man is defined first of all by his responsibility towards his brothers and towards history' (Vatican II, The Church Today, § 55). The revolutionary impact which this discovery should have for Christians, in Japan and throughout the Church, is that, as Vatican II has put it, 'the pivotal point of (religious) concern is man himself, whole and entire, body and soul, heart and conscience, mind and will' (*ibid.*, 3), and that this concern is innate to Japanese religious tradition.

I am seriously concerned about the influence of Western religious indifference upon the thousands of Japanese visitors in our midst. They have always learned, for better or for worse, through osmosis and eclectic integration. Western religious indifference while it shocks, also appeals to them.

The specific Christian contribution to the new humanism which the Japanese nation craves calls for a common effort to develop new communities of love and understanding, particularly in the wasteland of their and our urban centres. If Christians took their faith seriously and made man 'the pivotal point of their attention', they would want to post themselves at the centre of that polar field where Japan's religiosity, expressed in her quest for beauty, truth and goodness, meets God's eternal answer, Christ, manifested to a nation brought to the point at which existence flowers into redemption.

Anton Weiler

Theories About the
Causes of Religious Indifference

IN 1827 the Abbé Hugues Félicité Robert de Lamennais published the first volume of his four-volume work *Essai sur l'indifférence en matière de religion*. His view of the situation in which European society was placed at that time is clearly expressed in the Introduction to the book: 'The century that is really sick is not the one that is passionately involved in error, but the one that neglects and scorns truth. There is still power and consequently hope wherever violent outbursts occur, but what can be expected when there is no more movement, the pulse has ceased to beat and the heart is cold—only an imminent and inevitable break-up. It would be futile to try to hide from ourselves the fact that European society is rapidly approaching that end-point. The rumbling noises in its breast and the shocks that rack it are not the most frightening symptoms that are visible to the observer. The worst symptom is undoubtedly the lethargy, indifference and deep drowsiness into which it is clearly sinking—and who will rescue it?'

A century and a half before this, Jacques Bénigne Bossuet, the Bishop of Meaux and a famous preacher and polemicist, had foreseen the dangers threatening the Church in the form of Cartesian philosophy and a century after Lamennais the problem of religious indifference was systematically discussed by P. Richard in 1922 in the *Dictionnaire de Théologie Catholique*. Richard defined religious indifference as the 'attitude of those who do not decide between various forms of religion or who regard them all as of equal value'.

It is obvious from the distinctions that Richard made between negative and positive indifference and between absolute individual and absolute politico-social indifferentism and his use of such synonymous and equivalent terms as neutrality, tolerance and latitudinarianism that he, like Bossuet and Lamennais before him, approached the question from a dogmatic point of view. At the same time, however, he also dealt with what he called 'practical indifference', by which he meant the indifference of those who practised no religion at all, not on a more or less carefully thought-out rational basis, but simply because of habit. The causes to which he attributed religious indifference included a lack of information, frequently amounting to guilty ignorance, human passions such as sensuality, concupiscence and intellectual or moral independence and selfish worship of oneself and finally such factors as persistence in evil. The fact that those who are indifferent suppress their inborn ability to know God in this way and do not let their spirit do what it instinctively wants to do, namely raise itself up to the Lord of the physical and moral world, is central to this argument. If these obstacles are removed by a good religious education, if the passions are directed towards such loftier values as the good of the family, the Fatherland and humanity and towards a concern for artistic, moral or intellectual improvement and finally if man's natural religious instincts are stimulated by a constant emphasis on the ultimate purpose of life and the existence of a First Cause, then conversion is possible.

The rationalistic tendency of this analysis is at once apparent and the essence of the problem can be expressed by the following question: Is it possible for man to remain indifferent towards the great questions concerning his nature and his destiny? At the level of morality, this question can be expressed in the following way: Is there a God and do we have an obligation towards him; if so, what is our obligation?

Christian apologists were entrusted with the task of answering these questions and they had to take into account the factor of absolute religious indifferentism in the forms of atheism and irreligious deism. They responded to this task by pointing to the necessity of religion on the basis of *a priori* considerations, psychological factors concerning the need that man experienced in his spirit, will and heart for religion and historical arguments about the various forms of religion that man, who had always been religious in every part of the world, had produced. These apologists concluded that every man was bound to look for the one, true and supernatural religion, which was Christianity. They had, therefore, to combat indifferentism towards Christianity and stress the exclusive claim made by the Catholic Church to religious truth.

Sixty years after the appearance of Richard's article and despite the accumulated logic of rational arguments, the crusades conducted by the apologists, the continued war against sin and passion and a very purposeful system of Christian education, the Church has still not succeeded in overcoming religious indifference. I do not intend to provide a diagnosis of that indifference today—that can be found elsewhere in this issue of *Concilium*. I shall confine myself here to an attempt to identify the factors that are responsible for the intense and rapid growth of that indifference. The traditional answers in the tradition of Bussuet, Lamennais and Richard are no longer satisfactory, mainly because they lack a firm empirical and scientific basis. According to the outline provided by the editors of this issue of *Concilium*, an attempt must be made to look for whatever connection there may be between this indifferentism and the welfare society of the West, the disappearance of trust in the established churches and their representatives, the influence of the popularisation of various forms of the modern criticism of religion and our improved knowledge of the real nature of the great religions of mankind. It is also possible to add a number of other factors to this list of relationships. We can ask, for example, whether there is a relationship between indifferentism and a much more scientific process of education and a more scientific understanding of human psychology, the gradual disappearance of authoritarian attitudes, the non-authoritarian presentation of Christian faith to the younger generation, the relatively underdeveloped attitude of otherwise intellectually developed lay people towards theology, the (assumed?) irrelevance of Christianity in giving form to individual, social, economic and political life, the cultural revolution of the 1960s and 1970s among young people living at that time and the fact that the traditional orthodox faith and morality has in recent years not been stressed by the Church.

Research into relationships of this kind that are the result of everyday experience has to be empirical and scientific and consists of analyses of correlations that are based on representative statistics. It is possible to record the opinions of those questioned with regard to religion and matters that are relevant to religion, divide them into percentages of 'ayes', 'noes' and 'no opinion' and in this way form a picture of the spread of different opinions about these relationships. These opinions can then be related to various categories according to sex, age, social class, level of prosperity, political conviction, cultural and historical context, type of religion and religious denomination and so on. In this way, quite a detailed descriptive analysis can be made of the situation of religion in the Netherlands, or in Western Europe, for example.

Surveys of this kind will not, however, get us very far if we are trying to analyse the causes of religious indifference or to come to an understanding of the factor leading to the rapid growth of that indifference that has been statistically recorded. Opinions that are related to certain attitudes can be recorded, but it is not possible to show clearly why those questioned hold their opinions or behave in a certain way towards religion. The most that can be done is to group together a number of opinions after conducting surveys that are aimed to record opinions about possible relationships.

In the reflections that go together with statistical and analytical research into church membership and non-church membership and faith and lack of faith, it has again and again been pointed out that the causes that have been suggested have not usually been verified or, if they have, the generalised statements that have been made have often been refuted. One such statement that has proved to be no longer tenable is that a conservative attitude on the part of the Church leads to a reduction in active membership of the Church, because non-authoritarian members leave the Church when orthodoxy and a strict check on morals are emphasised. The very opposite seems in praxis to be the case: the conservative churches are, according to Dean M. Kelley at least, growing or are holding on to their members more successfully than the more tolerant churches. The preservation of older forms of Christian doctrine and praxis, supported by the formation of groups which reinforce identity, apparently appeals to people who feel that their mental state and their need for conservation and security are seriously violated by the extremely materialistic phenomena that exist in the welfare State and the consumer society and by the various aspects of crisis that occur during economic recession.

In outlining the attitudes of the kind of person who visits a conservative church when life proves too difficult for him, some attention has been given to the so-called contextual factors influencing his choice of religion and church membership. The social, cultural, economic and political climate in which he lives plays a very important part in determining his choice of position with regard to religion, but it does not in any sense provide a single and undifferentiated stimulus for human behaviour. What one man finds threatening, another finds liberating—one man seeks refuge in (or returns to) a conservative church while another avoids it. The same contextual phenomena are interpreted in a diametrically opposed way by both men.

The most all-embracing contextual thesis is that of secularisation, which has for a very long time been regarded as the most satisfactory way of explaining the phenomenon of alienation from the Church and the desacralisation of society. This thesis has, however, been increasingly rejected of late, partly because it does not really deal with the phenomena of a 'new religiosity' outside the framework of traditional faith and also because it is far too generalised.

As soon as we begin to look for more specific causes, it at once becomes apparent that any attempt to point to effective factors results in no more than a series of entirely or partly tautological reformulations of the phenomenon that is to be explained. Because of this, if the theses in question are not tautological, they are almost always hypotheses which are either unverified or have not been verified in a justifiable way. According to the religious sociologist, Walter Goddijn, this certainly applies to the following long list of possible factors which, it is claimed, have influenced the progress of the movement away from the Church: dissatisfaction with society and socialism, the derationalisation of the technology of production, the continued penetration of secular and scientific thinking into all spheres of life, the break-up of traditional forms of society by industrialisation and urbanisation and the change in man's relationships with his situation in life that is closely related to this, a more open resistance to authority and authoritarian attitudes, which is also expressed as opposition to the Church and those in authority in the Church, the emergence of all kinds of associations and the great expansion of leisure activities, the appearance of new means of communication, the secularisation of social care, the different social orientation of the churches and the integrating and stabilising influence of non-Church forms of organisation. This list consists of ten possible factors, but the theses which relate these factors to the phenomenon of the movement away from the Church and possibly also to the phenomenon of religious indifference are not validated in a scientific way. There are too may complicating factors for us to be able to imply that there are unequivocal relations.

Factors both within and outside the Church can play a part in the process of alienation from the Church. The causal operation of these factors is, however, unevenly distributed between religious groups and nations. Socio-economic circumstances, regional influences and the cultural context and specific historical background are, both generally and individually, related to each other in such a complex way that an analysis of these factors can only be really meaningful in the case of small and carefully selected analytical units of the size, for example, of a parish in a fishing village. The problems of methodology and scientific theory that arise when generalisations of this kind are made and then verified or falsified are so well known that extreme caution is always advisable.

I would like to give as an example of this a summary of some of the conclusions drawn from a scientific processing of a very recent national survey, conducted in 1979 in the Netherlands, into the phenomenon of secularisation and 'decolumnisation', which is the name given in the Netherlands to the breakdown of social structures built up on an earlier confessional basis. What emerged from this was that even the Netherlands could not be treated as a single unit for the purpose of analysis. There are as many as fifty-four faith groups in the country (compared with the United States, where there are 1,203!) and the differences in attitude between these groupings are quite significant. What is more, the Netherlands as a whole are also significantly different from other European nations.

Felling, Peters and Schreuder, who were responsible for this survey, paid special attention to the religious factor in the socio-cultural changes that have been observed in the Netherlands. The thesis that they wanted either to verify or falsify in their survey was this: In the past, religion and the churches made an important contribution to culture in the Netherlands, but today religion and the churches play only a marginal part in society. This thesis was tested out in a series of inquiries, but, if the individual nature of these processes of change are to be fully recognised, their context will have to be clarified by a long-term historical analysis.

This survey showed quite clearly that the thesis did not apply to the Netherlands, where there was, in 1979, still a very pronounced Christian consciousness or view of life and the world. It also showed that there are no large-scale alternatives competing with religion and the churches in the form of complexes of a secular, sceptical, agnostic or nihilistic kind. At the same time, however, it was also clear from the survey and its analysis that the Christian view of life and the world was now only third in order of cultural forces. In the Netherlands of 1979, a generalised and not specifically Christian belief in transcendence was stronger and the strongest conviction of all was that the meaning of life was to be found in this life itself and that you had to give meaning to it yourself.

Felling, Peters and Schreuder then tried to establish a link between these results and the active church membership or the non-church membership of the respondents, basing their conclusions on what those respondents told them about their attitude, that is, on their 'reported behaviour'. What emerged from this is that there is really a very clear division in the Netherlands between those who still belong to a church and those who do not and that this is expressed not only in their difference in conviction, but also in their attitude towards the Church. Those who regarded themselves as outside the Church (42 per cent) were in fact really outside it and for the most part attached no further importance to such rites as baptism, marriage and being buried. Those who still regarded themselves as members of a church on the other hand (58 per cent) took part in the services of that church and practised their religion. There was also one remarkable result that differed, in the opinion of Felling, Peters and Schreuder, from the conclusion drawn by Hans Mol and his collaborators from the investigation that they conducted in sixteen different countries in Northern, Western and Southern Europe. Mol encountered the same configuration in all these countries: a small percentage of non-church members, a minority (weak to strong) of active church members and a great mass of non-active members who nonetheless still kept to the transitional rites. The difference between the Netherlands and the pattern established by Mol and his collaborators in Europe can be explained on the basis of historical developments in the Netherlands. This specific situation cannot be adequately explained on the basis of social theoretical factors such as industrialisation, urbanisation and modernisation.

There would, then, seem to be a positive relationship between distance from the Church and Christianity and higher education and higher professional status and this relationship seems to apply to the tradition in the Netherlands. That tradition is also strikingly different from what is encountered in neighbouring countries. Those who conducted the survey in 1979 believe that the social conflict during the nineteenth and twentieth centuries that estranged the lower stratum of society from the Church and religion did not have the same result in the Netherlands because the churches there were socially deeply committed.

Another aspect of religion in the Netherlands to which Felling, Peters and Schreuder drew attention in 1979 is that there have been considerable differences between religious denominations. The various groups of strict orthodox Protestants (and particularly the Calvinist-Zwinglian Reformed Churches) have, in recent years, been able to maintain faith and church membership by means of their relatively closed Christian social organisations. There has, on the other hand, been a marked breakdown in the Catholic social organisations during the past twenty or so years and this has led to the disappearance of a number of structural guarantees of truth and certainty. The consequence of this has been that Catholics have far more doubts and uncertainties than members of the strict Reformed Churches in the Netherlands about the existence of God and the meaning of life, suffering and death.

Social surveys, analyses of situations and the processing of statistics, however, only reveal certain kinds of relationships. Comparative research is able to throw light on relevant contrasts in those patterns of relationships and these can sometimes be historically individually interpreted. Generalisations about relationships that are very frequently encountered in their different contexts may point to general socio-cultural conditions in which phenomena occur as religious indifference, but they do not reveal the causes of the increase that has been established in indifference to religion and/or the Church.

When there is a need to 'explain' in the social sciences, various explanatory models are constructed. The question then arises as to whether these models are plausible in the case of the phenomenon in question and, if so, which models are the most plausible. If there is insufficient scientifically verified certainty concerning the factors governing religious indifferentism, are there, then, any satisfactory explanatory models available which will provide theoretical constructions concerning the relevant relationships of a kind that a valuable insight can be gained into the processes observed?

It is perhaps important to re-establish what is meant by religion. The anthropologist Clifford Geertz has provided quite a good definition. It has often been used and it can serve as a point of departure here. According to Geertz, religion is (1) a system of symbols that functions (2) in order to establish powerful, compelling and long-lasting states and motivations in people by (3) expressing ideas about a universal existential order and by (4) investing those ideas with such an aura of factuality that (5) those dispositions and motivations give an impression of unanimous realism.

This description of religion contains a great number of elements that are interrelated and are well worth considering in connection with our search for a connection between the phenomenon of religious indifference and other phenomena. A number of theses can also be deduced from this description. One such thesis is, for example: If it is not possible to bring about a powerful, compelling and long-lasting disposition and motivation in people by means of the religious system of symbols, then that system is obviously not functioning as it should. This loss of function can develop at three levels, all of which are interrelated in Geertz's definition. It is valuable to examine each of these levels in turn.

In the first place, it is possible that the ideas expressed about a universal existential order or order of being no longer conform with people's pattern of experience or at least that those ideas and/or the official spokesmen of religion are no longer succeeding in establishing a sufficiently plausible and inspiring link between people's experience and interpretation of their order of being for them to construct a lasting spiritual attitude and motivation from it.

In the second place, it is possible that the failure has to be attributed above all to a shortcoming of the 'aura of factuality'—in other words, people who are indifferent to religion are not aware of the 'supernatural' reality as a reality behind the symbols. They are not deeply convinced that those symbols point to a reality that exists factually and they dismiss them as myths, inventions and primitive expressions of popular faith. In other words, religious realism, that is, the conviction that the 'supernatural' reality really *is* what the religious symbols and statements say it is, no longer functions properly. The cause of this loss of conviction regarding the supernatural reality may possibly be found in the spread of a concept of reality that is objective, scientific and rationalistic and can no longer be applied to the symbolic reality of religion. In other words, when they are measured against the norms of objectivistic scientism, universal metaphysical and religious concepts no longer have any value as reality.

In the third place, it is possible that the lack of a realistic basis for the norms of behaviour exposes spiritual motivation to moral indifferentism, because the symbolically presented 'factuality' of the supernatural and the natural order, from which those norms have to be derived, cannot be ascertained scientifically, that is, intersubjectively verifiably.

The failure of the religious system of symbols, as described by Geertz, to function properly can, in this analysis, be defined quite accurately as a loss of function, based on the fact that very many people no longer respond to religious realism. The attempts that have been made in recent years to overcome metaphysics and have resulted in such philosophies as materialism, existentialism, anti-logocentrism, nihilism and structuralism have inevitably undermined religious realism and the anti-essentialism, anti-conceptualism and anti-realism of many of these philosophical tendencies have certainly had an effect on the religious system of symbols of traditional Christian faith, that has been constructed on a foundation of realism. Modern theology, which has always taken man's experience of life today as its point of departure and has been very deeply influenced by these modern philosophical movements, has also contributed to this loss of function.

It is, however, clear that Geertz, who specialises in symbolic anthropology, is not claiming that religious realism is either correct or incorrect. All that he is doing is to point out its fundamental strength in the question of constructing an effective spiritual attitude both individually and socially. It is therefore important to note that the symbolic anthropological approach to the phenomenon of religion is not the only possible approach within the social sciences. There are other models which can be used for the purpose of explanation. The function of religion can be regarded as extending over a far wider field than simply the individual. Religion also has a social and political strength, in so far as its function with regard to and within society is concerned. Writing from the standpoint of functionalism, Emile Durkheim attributed a system-integrating function to religion and claimed that the relationship between the social and the political order was promoted by that function. Later functionalists followed him along that path.

Contemporary social scientists have confirmed that, seen from the point of view of a functionalist explanatory model, religion has certainly lost that systems-integrating function now and that all-embracing systems are constructed without reference to religion. Niklas Luhmann, while acknowledging this criticism of the functionalist approach to the phenomenon of religion and agreeing that it is often justified, has tried, in a systems theoretical analysis of the function of religion, to replace, in new terminology, the systems-integrating function of religion by referring to the relationships between system and environment and in so doing to attribute to religion the role of transforming the 'supernatural', as the 'environment' of the natural system, from indefinite to definite complexity, so that the natural social system is related in a graphic way to its supernatural environment. At the same time, the interpretative function which Geertz ascribed to religion has been extended by Luhmann from its purely individual sphere of activity to include a role in the construction of systems, which is one of the functions of religion in the processes of constituting meaning and significance. It has also been established that, if faith has become a purely private matter and there is no direct link between the social order of a culturally pluriform society and various religious convictions, as is the case in a secular or secularised State, those social and Church systems are no longer based on the ultimate certainty of a religious realism that is accepted by the whole of society, but are bound to become open human constructions.

The systems theoretical variant of the functionalist model provides us with an insight into the dynamism of systems constructions and transformations in relation to an environment, but the specific part played by people in the concrete who construct their society and their Church in their daily lives and activities and who are guided in this or not guided in it by religious convictions is not at the centre of the explanatory model, as is also the case in other functionalist theories. But people are not simply actors playing parts and action is not simply carrying out in reality a model that has no more than a descriptive status. People are consciously acting and motivated beings. And if they reject religion in constructing their motivation, there is always a loss of function in religion and that loss concerns people.

The question about the causes of religious indifference can therefore be expressed in the following way: Why do people reject the religious system of symbols? At the level of knowledge, it is possible that realism as a primary attitude has had to take second place in competition with an increasingly scientific mode of thinking in which nominalistic and conceptualistic presuppositions are used and the best scientific results are produced, in the empiristic and scientistic sense, by quantitative analytical methods. This increasing emphasis on scientific thought has worked its way through the schools and the mass media so that it has come to have a very important influence on the cognitive habitus, which is the mode of thinking that sustains 'common sense', and has even deprived it of its primary realism.

At the level of practical action, however, religious indifferentism is present in a most striking way. The Christian message is often regarded as irrelevant in the case of practical activity. We are expected to depend on our own constructive powers in our attempts to solve national, international and world-wide problems of unemployment, failing supplies of sources of energy, the arms race and the high mortality rate in certain countries. Christians' personal motivation and orientation towards values are neither greater nor smaller in such matters than those of humanists. All that can be said is that the earlier form of religious realism is clearly irrelevant in our present circumstances and our need to solve problems that go far beyond the private sphere or any sectarian interest. People, then, are expected to make their own history and in this they have no supernatural blueprint or plan at their disposal. This in fact would seem to be the 'discovery of man', the new Renaissance and it is taking place without reference to God. A second cause of religious indifference today can therefore be found in our experience of the practical irrelevance of the Christian message.

A possible objection to this is that the myth of responsible, self-conscious, motivated and convinced man as the subject, the bearer and the builder of his own history and his own future has been superseded. Even though religion and religious realism may continue to motivate certain people, all socio-political and cultural developments are, in the opinion of certain scholars, ultimately determined by many different kinds of unconscious structural forces. Marx demonstrated that this was so in the case of the economic infrastructure that was developed during the important phases in the social organisation of production. Freud pointed to very much the same phenomenon in the development of the psychological structures of the individual personality. Claude Lévi-Strauss did the same for the transhistorical system of codes governing the construction of societies and their cultures and Michel Foucault defined the anonymous power structures which eventually produce the disciplined and trained men that the future needs.

Following Foucault's analysis, it is possible to say that those anonymous forces are the cause of present-day religious indifference in people and this is because the greatest possible tolerance with regard to private faith is encouraged as a principle in the formation of societies and States. The national and international set of rules, within which the solution or at least the control of the countless appalling world problems has to be found, calls for people who are indifferent to religion and who are no longer influenced by that religious realism that leads to an exclusive and totalitarian dream of a world State founded on a basis of religious salvation. The exclusion of those who think differently is something that cannot be accepted in the construction of a new economic and political order, with the result that there is a need today of people who are indifferent to religion. It is clear, for example, from the religious fanaticism of the spiritual leaders in modern Iran that religious realism and fundamentalism is diametrically opposed to the development of modern democratic society.

The different forms of structuralist interpretation of reality, however, eliminate people as acting subjects, at least in their explanatory models, to such a degree that there has for some time now been a reaction to this among social scientists in the form of a theory directed towards praxis. They have, however, encountered serious problems of methodology in forming this theory and in analysing religious indifferentism as an element of practical action in a way that is similarly directed towards praxis. It would seem that there is a great need for caution with regard to possible realistic and objectivistic presuppositions. In carrying out a scientific analysis that bears the imprint of these options, the researcher is, at least in his methodology, separated from the object of his study. Religious praxis, in the sense of religious actions and explicitly religiously inspired social activity, presents itself in such cases as a kind of spectacle or play and an attempt can be made to ascertain the rules and the distribution of roles and to decode the language used in that play. But when that happens, the researcher is in danger of forgetting that he will insert his own concerns and principles of knowledge into the territory that he is studying and will in this way give it a form that corresponds to his questions.

This problem is not solved by adopting the so-called 'emic'[1] approach, that is, the approach of the one who either carries out or stands at a distance from religious praxis. The primary and non-reflective 'truth' of the first state of becoming aware of and the first submission to the spiritual intensity and intentionality of religious praxis is undoubtedly a point of reference for scientific knowledge, but it does not in itself include scientific, that is, critically verifiable, intersubjective knowledge. Even structuralist hermeneutics can adapt themselves to objective demands, if those demands do not concern the intentions of the subject in his religious activity, but only call, for example, for the economic or linguistic relationships which structure religious practice and the symbols that accompany it. Neither primary, experienced knowledge nor scientific structural knowledge is in itself sufficient. What is involved here is the concept of the practical relationships between those primary experiences and the 'objective', that is, the structures that are literally 'thrown in the way'. Also involved is a knowledge of the practical conditions that make these relationships either possible or impossible and a knowledge of the human and social states on the basis of which these so-called structures are made present and reproduced by people.

Pierre Bourdieu has pointed to the way in which a theory of this praxis that makes this kind of knowledge possible can be developed, by concentrating on the generative principle that is present and active in the carrying out of that praxis. What is involved here is not an analysis of man's living experience or any kind of subjectivism, but a knowledge of the conditions that make the production of knowledge—in this case religious knowledge—possible and the functioning of that knowledge in practical association with life both at the individual and at the social level and in the development of cultural and political dominance systems.

Bourdieu has focused his attention on the state, disposition or habitus that has been cultivated, firmly inculcated, built up in the earliest childhood and again and again reinforced in the individual within the group, on the basis of which all praxis is developed and formed as a small set of generative patterns of thought and behaviour. He is concerned above all with a knowledge of the dispositional structures that govern both praxis and its accompanying ideas, including the religious symbols. The habitus and ethics that are inculcated into people are, as experience that has become a structure, the basis of the formation and evaluation of all the experiences that follow and therefore also the basis of all practical activity.

That activity is changed when the 'objective' social conditions of the production of knowledge in relation to the reproduction of that habitus change and the shared systems of ideas, with their 'objective' social consensus concerning the significance and the roots of explicitly order-affirming actions, collapse. The dispositional system, which has changed historical experience into 'nature', is the principle of continuity and regularity of praxis and also of transformation, when, in a changing situation of crisis, it is no longer possible to obtain an adequate response from the professional and practical assentors to the system of symbols that has been valid until that time and the reproduction of the habitus has ceased. The failure of those professionals in the system of symbols—Church leaders and theologians—is to a very great extent the result of their own defective knowledge of the social reality in which 'their' people live, a reality which develops on its own in relative autonomy and very often without being recognised.

The habitus is clearly no match, in a situation of revolutionary change, for the challenge presented by the new situation. At the same time, however, it is not possible for it to return to its previous structural and functional disposition. Practical mastery of the symbolic order is thereby lost. The habitus, which is in this case religious, is disrupted and no longer operates generatively and as a means of bringing about unity in the construction of the existence of the individual and society. The symbolical relationships that have served to legitimate the socio-political reality also lose their validity when the habitus is disrupted. They lose their practical coherence because the habitual praxis has lost its mastery of the social situation.

Bourdieu has, in describing the habitus as the generative source of praxis, pointed to an explanation that can also be applied with some relevance to the emergence and growth of religious indifference. (It is also worth noting that the concept 'habitus' is a very old one that is found in Aristotle and Thomas Aquinas.) In Bourdieu's theory, a connection can be made between the two previously mentioned causes of religious indifferentism, namely the loss of religious realism in the sphere of knowledge and the experience of the practical irrelevance of Christianity. My thesis is that, if religious indifference occurs on a large scale, the habitus that is originally informed by a religious realism is disrupted and can therefore no longer function socially and politically, because it is clear to people that an adequate social system cannot be developed or kept in being with such a religious system of symbols. Despite all the preaching, denominational schools, encyclicals, all the insistence on frequent communion and confession, all the eucharistic congresses and confessional organisations—including those responsible for Catholic and Protestant broadcasting and the religious press—it is clear that the inculcated habitus has not proved equal to the pressure of rapidly changing historical, socio-cultural, economic, demographic and political circumstances in the West over the past decades, that is, during the 1960s and 1970s.

Religious realism still functions in the totalitarian regimes in Christian Latin America and Christian Africa as a divine justification of a system of unity imposed by force. This kind of religious realism is fortunately no longer effective in the West, where rationalism and the Enlightenment have led to the democratisation and secularisation of society, despite a relatively brief intermezzo of National Socialist and Fascist totalitarianism with its fatal results, although it has to be admitted that neo-conservative movements do seem to be aiming to reconfessionalise society and to be making use of religious realism and fundamentalism in the Christian system of symbols in order to impose them as the only true interpretation of religious values.

It is also quite important to take a wider spectrum into consideration in any attempt to formulate a theory, since indifference is not confined simply to religion. Even the non-religious secular system of symbols used in a rationalist view of life and the world is set aside in so far as it is realistic. Our conviction that a better world can be produced on the basis of reason alone has been fundamentally shattered. There is no longer any real need to attack the errors of rationalism and idealism with apologetic arguments. They have been refuted, in recent decades, by such things as Auschwitz, Hiroshima, Vietnam and the accumulated threat of nuclear destruction. Reason can, in other words, no longer be regarded as the autonomous constitutive force in the construction of society. It has in fact been reduced to the level of a force used in the systems theoretical techniques of planning and the building of econometric models. The new scientific and technological form of rationalism can to a very great extent be expressed in terms of quantitative social and economic relationships. It is seen basically as fairness and is applied almost exclusively to the moral and/or political acceptability of the distribution of welfare and incomes on a world-wide scale.

It is also clear that Christianity has become irrelevant in praxis partly because man appears to have lost control in the task of building up society and because there is no longer any enthusiasm for a society that is quantitatively regulated. Both these phenomena have made young people especially look for an alternative that is either mystical or active and may perhaps also be religious. Not everyone wants to live and act on the basis of a purely economic interest, to devote himself to the accumulation of profit and to become a slave of an economically regulated society.

Religious realism has been superseded by a new form of theological hermeneutics, in which an attempt is made to provide new answers to the questions that people are asking today because they are unsure of their own existence and are individually indifferent, believing that it 'simply does not matter'. Those who are developing this new hermeneutical approach are trying to speak with inspiration and to arouse a trust in the Holy Spirit. They want people to abandon their earlier realistic and metaphysical certainty and to redevelop a new religious habitus based on courage and hope.

At the same time, however, despite all attempts to formulate a new theology, religious indifferentism is still on the increase. Is it such a traumatic experience to abandon the earlier attitudes of faith and to let go of cognitive certainty that we are not bold and hopeful enough to accept the uncertainty of faith? Do people have such an overwhelming sense of impotence with regard to the great complexity of modern society and its structures that even privatised religion does not 'liberate' them? It is possible that they will only cease to be indifferent to religion when the realistic features and the factuality of Geertz's definition of religion are no longer applicable to Christian faith and these have been completely replaced by a new religious habitus of indestructible trust in God that is stronger than the darkness of the metaphysical anonymity of the divine element and the inhumanity of man's existence.

Translated by David Smith

Note.

1. Emics refers to a variety of theoretical field approaches in anthropology concerned with the inside or native (folk) view of a culture. The concept is based on the formulation of Kenneth Pike (1954), who proposed that a model for studying non-linguistic behaviour be devised analogous to the phonetic and phonemic approaches in linguistic theory—hence 'emic' and 'etic'. *Encyclopedia of Anthropology*, eds. David E. Hunter and P. L. Witten, New York 1976, p. 142.—See also Kenneth Pike *Language in Relation to a Unified Theory of the Structure of Human Behaviour*, I, Glendale, Ca., Summer Institute of Linguistics, 1954.

Bibliography

The following books and articles have been consulted: J. E. Barnhart *The Study of Religion and its Meaning. New Explorations in the Light of Karl Popper and Emile Durkheim* (Religion and Reason 12) (The Hague, Paris, New York 1977); Robert N. Bellah *Beyond Belief. Essays on Religion in a Post-Traditional World* (New York 1970); Pierre Bourdieu *Outline of a Theory of Practice* (Cambridge 1977); Martin Buber *Gottesfinsternis. Betrachtungen zur Beziehung zwischen Religion und Philosophie* (Zürich 1953); C. Campbell 'Analysing the Rejection of Religion' *Social Compass* 24 (1977) 339-346; Walter H. Caps *Ways of Understanding Religion* (New York 1972); Richard E. Creel *Religion and Doubt. Toward a Faith of your Own* (Englewood Cliffs 1977); Jean Delumeau *Le Christianisme va-t-il mourir?* (Paris 1977); Mary Douglas 'The Effects of Modernization on Religious Change' *Daedalus* (Winter 1982) 1-19; Louis Dupré *The Other Dimension. A Search for the Meaning of Religious Attitudes* (New York 1972); David L. Edwards *Religion and Change* (London 1969); 'What is Religion? An Enquiry for Christian Theology' eds. Mircea Eliade and David Tracy *Concilium* 136 (6/1980); A. Felling, J. Peters and O. Schreuder 'Gebroken identieit. Een studie over christelijk en onchristelijk Nederland *Archief voor de Geschiedenis van de Katholieke Kerk in Nederland* 24 (1982) 25-81; Clifford Geertz 'Religion as a

Cultural System' *The Interpretation of Cultures. Selected Essays* (New York 1973) pp. 87-125, originally published in *Anthropological Approaches to the Study of Religion* ed. M. Banton (London 1966) pp. 1-46; W. Goddijn *et al. Hebben de Kerken nog toekomst? Commentaar op het onderzoek 'Opnieuw: God in Nederland'* (Annalen van het Thijmgenootschap 69/1) (Baarn 1981); Andrew M. Greeley *The Persistence of Religion* (London 1973); Dean M. Kelley *Why Conservative Churches are Growing. A Study in Sociology of Religion* (New York 1977); Gerhard Lenski *The Religious Factor. A Sociological Study of Religion's Impact on Politics, Economics and Family Life* (New York 1963); Niklas Luhmann *Funktion der Religion* (Frankfurt am Main 1977); *Western Religion. A Country by Country Sociological Inquiry* (Religion and Reason 2) ed. Hans Mol (The Hague, Paris and New York 1972); *ibid. Identity and Religion, International, Cross-Cultural Approaches* ed. Hans Mol (London 1978); Adriaan Peperzak 'The Meaning of Religion in Contemporary Western Society' *Dialectics and Humanism* 4 (1980) 69-93; Karl Rahner *et al. Ist Gott noch gefragt? Zur Funktionslosigkeit des Gottesglaubens* (Düsseldorf 1973); *Religion als Problem der Aufklärung: eine Bilanz aus der religionstheoretischen Forschung* ed. Trutz Rendtorff (Göttingen 1980); *Religion, érudition et critique à la fin du XVIIe siècle et au début du XVIIIe* (Paris 1968); *Religion. Ein Jahrhundert theologischer, philosophischer, soziologischer und psychologischer Interpretationsansätze* ed. Christoph Elsas (Munich 1975); *The New Religious Consciousness* eds. Charles Y. Glock and Robert N. Bellah (Berkeley 1976); *Der Religionswandel unserer Zeit im Spiegel der Religionswissenschaft* ed. Günther Stephenson (Darmstadt 1976); *Ways of Being Religious. Readings for a New Approach to Religion* eds. Frederick J. Streng, Charles L. Lloyd Jnr. and Jay T. Allan (Englewood Cliffs 1973); R. J. Zwi Werblowsky *Beyond Tradition and Modernity. Changing Religions in a Changing World* (London 1976); Bryan Wilson *Contemporary Transformations of Religion* (London 1976).

PART II

Some Provisional Interpretations

Willy Obrist

Indifference to Religion: Symptom of a Mutation of Consciousness

ARE PEOPLE only indifferent to religion, or to religious feeling as well? Do they still cling to Christianity and only turn away from the church, or do they think they can find salvation in other religions or movements similar to religion? Are people looking for religious sentiment apart from religion or are they no longer bothered about this either? Probably all this is the case.

1. SEEING INDIFFERENCE ONLY AS A SYMPTOM

Indifference is a complex phenomenon. But if the Church wants to get behind it, it must first see it squarely, simply as a phenomenon: as a symptom indicating that there are many people to whom the Church with its kerygma can no longer get through. In the art of medicine it is frowned on to treat symptoms. The rule there is that treatment should only be drawn up when one has grasped the process which is at the root of the symptoms. So the proper thing seems to be to inquire about this change in general consciousness which appears as indifference. In doing so one will have to accept the fact that many of those who are indifferent have correctly recognised the 'signs of the times'—albeit unconsciously—and that the Church itself will have to change its attitude in fundamental matters if it wishes to do justice to what it calls its mission.

2. THE MODERN EPISTEMOLOGICAL REVOLUTION

Nowadays it is a commonplace to say that Western man's understanding of himself and of the world has changed fundamentally since the middle ages. But what this change *at root consists in* is less obvious.

First of all we must realise that in modern times—outside Church and theology, and hardly noticed by them—an epistemological revolution of gigantic proportions has taken place, in two stages.

To grasp the germ of this revolution we should not look to the history of philosophy. First, because the really significant changes have occurred outside philosophy, but secondly because the history of philosophy lags behind the development: because so far it has hardly taken cognisance of the second stage of the epistemological revolution, which is of burning interest if we are to understand what, for the Church, is the positive aspect of indifference.

To get closer to the issue we must consider *modern science*. But we must not look primarily at its most obvious achievements—the multiplication of knowledge about nature and civilisation. What has revolutionised our world-view are the incidental 'by-products' of the concern for increased knowledge. If we ask why modern research (compared, for example, with the Greeks' attempts) has been so successful, we come up against the urge which arose with the Renaissance to *penetrate layer by layer behind the façade of the mere appearance*: no longer to ask speculatively about the *prima causa* but to trace the *secondary* causes of phenomena, using the apparatus of modern empiricism which was available for the first time at this level of consciousness. The aim was research into nature and civilisation. This produced, as a by-product, the *insight that the spontaneous impression furnished by our systems of perception is illusory*. It was this insight which radically altered our understanding of ourselves and the world.

In speaking of perception we think first of all—as children of the positivistic generation—of sense-perception. Besides sense-perception, however, which archaic man often called 'seeing with the eyes of the body', he also knew another kind of perception: 'seeing with the eyes of the soul'. By this he meant what he perceived in dreams and visions. In both kinds of perception the spontaneous impression was found to be illusory, but in different ways. And it was primarily the change in understanding this 'seeing with the eyes of the soul' which led to our conceiving ourselves and the world in a way quite different from that of archaic man, and hence, too, different from that of man at the time when the Christian religion arose and began to spread.

3. 'SEEING WITH THE EYES OF THE BODY' IS RELATIVISED

From the beginning of modern times until far into the nineteenth century the scientist's interest was applied only to what was perceivable by the *senses*, whether natural phenomena or evidence of civilised creativity. *Methodological* positivism became the scientist's ethos: its fundamental axiom was that only what could be perceived by the senses could be regarded as scientifically proved.

Research in the natural sciences using instruments and indirect methods eventually led to the insight that the world is different from how it appears to us in spontaneous sense-impression; that in the first place our sense-perception systems can receive only a limited selection of signals, and moreover that they are only suitable for perceiving the middle range of dimensions, not the micro- and macro-realms. Recent biological research into evolution has shed light on to why this is so by showing how cognitive systems from amoeba to man—in order to survive—have developed step by step by 'pattern-matching' to their environment (evolutionary epistemology).

However, the insight that the world is different from our perception of it evolved by such small steps that very few people have become aware of what a revolution this implies over against the archaic understanding of nature based on spontaneous sense-impression. In spite of the huge expansion of consciousness which this first stage of the epistemological revolution brought about—hand in hand with the increase of knowledge—it has done nothing to change the accepted view that with our senses (apart from proprioception) we perceive things *outside* ourselves.

4. 'SEEING WITH THE EYES OF THE SOUL' IS RELATIVISED

Inquiring what lay behind 'seeing with the eyes of the soul' produced quite different consequences for the accepted understanding of the world. This did not begin until the second half of the nineteenth century, but at the beginning of the present century it led to a breakthrough. Here the insight that the spontaneous impression is illusory caused the *world-view to rotate through 180 degrees*: a part of objective reality which, since the

Stone Age, people had apperceived as something existing externally and had imagined—in different ways in different cultures—as a metaphysical world, was now seen to be something internal to the soul.

The change in apperception of 'seeing with the eyes of the soul' came about through the development of *empirical* psychology. This arose in the womb of the natural sciences. So it approached phenomena of the soul in the manner developed by scientific research and took over from the earlier, largely speculative psychology. Initially it was only interested in the consciousness, since, for positivism, what people in archaic times times had called the soul was reduced to consciousness. Fantasies, dreams and visions were regarded as the result of the activity of the consciousness.

In time, however, observations were made which could not be explained by the paradigm of consciousness-psychology. Apart from what we now call parapsychological phenomena, these were mainly religious conversation experiences, which were on the increase due to revivalism. It was observed that in each case the conversions had come after a fairly long period of preparation, of which the person concerned had not been aware. Conversion suddenly erupted into consciousness like a ripe fruit. On the basis of similar observations people postulated the existence of an unconscious psyche (i.e., not directly available to consciousness). For a long time, however, there was no way of demonstrating the existence and functioning of the unconscious.

Sigmund Freud had a first methodological success. His method was that of free association and dream analysis. He was able to prove that dreams were not created by consciousness or its 'centre', the Ego, but were *perceived* by the Ego as finished products. Without knowing it, Freud had extended the prevailing concept of knowledge and overcome the positivism of its world-view.

However, the model of the unconscious psyche which Freud constructed was provisional and incomplete. Soon afterwards it was replaced by the more refined model of C. G. Jung. Using a new method (controlled association and amplification) Jung showed that the unconscious is much wider than Freud had thought; moreover that it has a governing centre like consciousness, and that this 'centre' (the Self) controls the integral development of the whole psyche, including consciousness: it provides the conscious Ego with corrective, meaning-giving and creative impulses, and these messages reach the Ego—depending on the state of consciousness—as waking fantasies, sudden 'insights', as dreams and visions.

A further achievement of Jung's was to have deciphered the language of the unconscious. He showed that the unconscious Self communicates with the conscious Ego largely through a language of images, i.e., that the images and forms seen in dreams and visions are *linguistic formulas* by means of which the unconscious illustrates things which cannot be shown directly and mostly cannot be formulated conceptually. This meant that the spontaneous impression given in the archaic 'seeing with the eyes of the soul' was also illusory. To what extent, one can see by examining visions. In analysis one is relatively often concerned with visionaries and has opportunity to explore the phenomenon in detail. Unlike dreams, a person is visited by visions while awake. Externally one cannot communicate with him. He no longer reacts to sense stimuli and is often in a deeply comatose condition. Subjectively, however, he feels awake, more so that usual. He seems to be seeing something taking place *outside* himself. Landscape, people, events—all seem real to him.

This spontaneous impression arises because the internal stream of perception flowing from the unconscious Self to the conscious Ego *is projected externally* without the Ego being involved or even being aware of it. What is perceived as a result of this spontaneous impression is called a *concretist* understanding. At an earlier stage in the development of consciousness, the content of dreams too, especially the 'big' dreams, was apperceived in a concretist sense, a fact that is still observable in primitive peoples.

For Western man with his highly-developed consciousness this 'spontaneous impression' now only applies to visions.

5. THE ARCHAIC UNDERSTANDING OF SELF AND THE WORLD

We call the understanding of self and the world which resulted from belief in the spontaneous impression of 'seeing with the eyes of the soul', i.e., the concretist apperception of something internal, 'archaic' or 'mythical'. But the myth is only part of the archaic view of the world. There was also, in the early stages, the experience of participation, i.e., an almost physical sense of relatedness to all things, hand in hand with a restricted Ego-development; there was the dynamist conception of space and of things, the 'presentist' experience of time and the general lack of causal thinking. All these elements declined greatly, however, in the wake of the evolution of consciousness, even during the archaic period. The mythical 'dimension' remained longest intact, but even this was far more prominent in the early stages of development than towards the end of the archaic world-view, when it was still alive only in the realm of the Church. Once people realised that the spontaneous impression was illusory even in the case of the 'eyes of the soul', there was no longer a basis for this last vestige of the archaic understanding of the world.

Depth-psychology, however, has not only led to the abolition of these mythical vestiges. It also gave us the means of understanding mythical models of the world and the behaviour-patterns associated with them.

Research into projection showed us that whenever the Ego asks itself questions which it cannot answer with the cognitive means at its disposal, inner perceptions, largely illustrative of psychic states, are projected outwards. In the case of questions about nature, waking fantasies are chiefly projected. But since the projection process operates unconsciously, the Ego cannot recognise them as fantasies and takes them to be knowledge.

In this way, in archaic times, there arose mythical cosmologies and cosmogonies, mythical accounts of man's origins, of the origins of animals and plants, mythical anatomies, physiologies and pathologies, and a largely mythical chemistry (alchemy). Where questions about a people's past arose before the historico-critical method was available, mythical or mythically-tinged historical traditions arose, of which the Old Testament is a classical example.

These aetiological and historical myths were already replaced by empirical knowledge partially during the archaic period itself and then totally in modern times. The demythologisation of nature and history was a further by-product of modern (positivistic) research. Religious myths in the strict sense, however, have persisted into most recent times. It is these which are of interest to us in the context of indifference. We must study their origins more closely.

Since archaic man was unable to realise that the spontaneous impression in vision was illusory, the reports of visionaries were to him undubitable statements about real persons, things and historical events. On this basis he was convinced that besides 'this' world there was 'another' world, normally invisible, inhabited by concrete beings.

Archaic man recognised two categories of invisible people: those who had always been such (autochthonous metaphysical beings) and those who had once lived as human beings (the dead who 'live on'). Both of these appeared to him in dream and vision, and since he understood the symbolic creations of the interior stream of perception in a concretist sense, he 'knew' with inerrant certainty that those whom he 'saw' existed. Since the vision engenders a quite extraordinarily vivid sense of reality, and since it causes the superior power of the unconscious Self over the Ego to be experienced to a unique degree, archaic man believed that the 'other' beings were superior to those living in 'this' world. He believed that they could affect 'this' world. This was not conceived in our causal manner which is the product of science, but as direct intervention by mere thought and will. Therefore the miracle (in the theological sense) was something quite native to that view of the world. Through the experience of dream and vision one 'knew', furthermore, that the 'other beings' could communicate with man. This kind of communication was called revelation, and all knowledge of the 'other world' was ascribed to a process of revelation. What was 'revealed' to the visionary became the crystallisation-point for the formation of religious myths, the myths which became part of the 'deposit of faith' of the religion, both of tribal religion and of the high religions which include Christianity.

6. THE CHALLENGE TO TRUTHFULNESS

In Church circles it is still like breaking taboo when one speaks of the Christian myths, although the historico-critical study of the Bible has shown how they have acquired their shape: how the belief that Jesus had been raised was based on a vision (!) on the part of Peter, how it was only after his death that the idea that Jesus was the Messiah began to spread in the original Palestinian community, where the Messiah was still understood as a human being. This research also showed that the idea of the Messiah (Christos) as a heavenly being arose in the Jewish diaspora and only entered the Christian myth through the missionary activity of diaspora Jews; finally that the equation of this Christ (now seen as a heavenly being) with the Logos (an idea of Hellenistic provenance) as the consubstantial Son of the transcendent God was only formed in the womb of the Gentile-Christian communities. Comparative religious studies made it clear that this 'message about Jesus' was composed exclusively of mythological units such as occur in other cultures too: the consubstantial Son sent by the Father; the incarnation by virgin birth; the inconspicuous birth and wanderings of a divine being who brings mankind a new law and a new revelation; the element of suffering, death and resurrection, coupled with that of the redemptive, sacrificial death of the God, etc.

The method of redaction-criticism has shown how the evangelists went about historicising the Christian myth and projecting it on to the person of Jesus. Thus for example, 'Mark' created scenarios for the inherited corpus of words of Jesus, welding these together with stories which had come down separately, according to his own plan of space and time, into that 'Life of Jesus' which was regarded as a historical account for many generations; moreover, utterances of the Christian myth—most notably those of 'John'—have actually been put into the mouth of Jesus, to be subsequently believed as Jesus' own words.

These issues are known to all enlightened theologians. They are careful to keep them quiet. In raising them here and 'calling a spade a spade' I am calling for truthfulness. For our aim is to find out what lies behind the rapid growth of indifference and how the Church ought to react. The first thing one must do is to stop closing one's eyes to obvious facts. In the second step forward of the epistemological revolution, modern science (which in its first phase was closed or even hostile to religion) demonstrated that religious feeling is part of man's nature. But since it has also led to the superseding of the mythical world-view, it should be in the Church's interests—for the sake of survival—to discover what was the abiding core of the religious feeling of the past, and what was merely its archaic garb. The latter must be relinquished, giving place to a concept and form of religious feeling which corresponds to the modern level of consciousness and can be adopted by modern man without betraying his intellectual honesty. This must be borne in mind in what follows.

7. RITUAL AND THEOLOGY AS A VESTIGIAL EXPRESSION OF THE ARCHAIC

Myths, understood in a concretist sense, were assimilated to consciousness in two ways: by 'enacting' them in ritual and by reflecting upon them.

The enacting of ritual—this typically archaic behaviour pattern—consisted in a dramatisation of scenes from the myths concentrated into symbols. The myth was enacted by celebrants whose task was to go through it using precisely determined words and gestures. The assumption was that the myth's content was being repeated at the moment of its enactment, i.e., 'now' (because of the 'presentist' experience of time). The celebrant (priest) was seen as a being with a great power over things, yet at the same time people 'knew' that it was not he but the metaphysical beings which effected the salvation achieved by the ritual. Thus the ritual can be described as effecting something with the help of metaphysical beings; it is therefore seen in a different category from earlier 'magic'.

Theology (understood as dogmatics, primitive exegesis and morals) came about through reflection upon religious myth viewed in a concretist manner. Every theology—both of tribal religion and of the high religions—was based on the idea (which was part of the archaic world-view) that its myths were revealed by metaphysical beings and contained true affirmations about the world beyond and its relation to man.

What fundamental theologian today acknowledges the fact that this fundamental principle no longer holds? Who recognises, on the basis of the great step forward in the evolution of consciousness, the resultant *new conception* of the process which archaic man understood as supernatural revelation?

8. THE MUTATION OF CONSCIOUSNESS

Seen from this point of view of the *evolution* of consciousness, i.e., of the cumulative complexity of consciousness, the process I have described as an epistemological revolution is shown to be a *macro-mutation*. It is comparable to those great, irreversible leaps in biological evolution through which a new and more complex type of living organism came about, e.g., the leap from reptiles to mammals.

In the course of the evolution of consciousness this was the first macro-mutation. From the Stone Age up to the end of the middle ages the development had been in a *straight line*, resulting in *ever more complex mythical views of the world*. The 'other world' which originally had been assumed to be directly at hand, moved more into the background. The 'other beings' which originally were represented just as crassly physically as the topography of the 'other world', came to be invisaged more and more spiritually. Magical customs—effecting events by prophetic enactment and utterance—which were still an expression of the almost total lack of emancipation from the environment, and the consequent concepts of participation and the dynamist view of space, receded more and more in favour of ritual. In time the creation rituals, which were designed to preserve a world still felt to be unstable from sinking back into chaos, as well as the cultural rituals (for the success of hunting, cultivation and hand-crafts), were replaced by rituals intended to achieve the soul's welfare. This development reached its acme in the sacramental rites of the Catholic Church.

A significant *result* of the evolution of consciousness along with archaic apperception was the matter/spirit pair of concepts. The idea of matter was of course rather primitive, but that of spirit—in the form of metaphysical systems—was highly differentiated. *The archaic concept of spirit was developed by 'de-materialising' the 'other world'.* This undertaking bore its own limitations within it, for ultimately the idea of the spiritual was asymptotically approaching a frontier which, with archaic apperception, could not be crossed: the purely spiritual being, i.e., the general concept which exists independently of consciousness and things (conceptual realism). The development could proceed only if a fundamentally new concept of the spiritual came into being. No doubt this was one of the main reasons for the occurrence of the mutation. Now, for an understanding of indifference to religion it is significant that the mutation was carried through as a dialectical process, a process known in the development of the individual consciousness as the law of opposing tensions yielding a transcending function.

When the first step was taken, leading to the relativising of sense-impressions, people began to catch up on knowledge of the 'material world' which up to then had been underdeveloped. Whereas the archaic world-view continued to be cultivated in the Church, outside it, as we have seen, a demythologisation of nature and history took place. In addition, what began as a methodological positivism became more and more an ideological one: a restricted view of the world which refused to accept anything not perceptible by the senses. Since the positivist suppressed inner perception, he blocked up the source of religious feeling, ethical norms and meaning. Thus at the end of the nineteenth century there was a genuine opposition between two irreconcilable ways of understanding oneself and the world. In this field of tension the mutation's decisive second step could take place. When researchers, suffering under this tension, rediscovered inner perception at the same time as it became clear that it would have to be apperceived in a new way, the breakthrough occurred. A new, once again complete world-view was there, uniting the opposing views at a higher level.

The new world-view is no longer dualistic like the archaic, nor monistic like extreme positivism (materialism), but unistic and nuanced. This became possible because of the *achievement of the complementary way of thought*. This new thought can cope, on the one hand, with consciousness's necessity, in virtue of its structure, of apperceiving in opposing pairs of concepts; yet it can grasp reality unistically. In the new world-view matter and spirit, body and soul are seen simply as two *complementary aspects* of the spatio-temporal reality which is in itself unitary. If we regard this reality, alone available to us, in its material aspect, it presents itself as energy in the sense of physics. Seen in its spiritual aspect, it appears as a striving forward along the time-axis towards an ever more complex arrangement of energy and an ever-increasing inwardness of the resultant spatio-temporal forms.

The question of the 'arranger', which has always led to the 'God of the philosophers' is fully justified in this world-view, but affirmations about him, here more than ever, must remain in the terms of *theologia negativa*. However, contrary to this concept of the transcendent creator-God, which has always been the result of reflection, the idea of the God-who-reveals-himself (an idea acquired through direct experience) was transposed into the psychic dimension—into man's 'interiority'—by the mutation of consciousness.

By this interiority is understood the puzzling ability of living beings to have experiences, emotions, moods, to recognise, know and decide. All beings lower down the evolutionary ladder than man are not aware of themselves: from man's point of view they are unconscious. But what biology, and particularly the study of behaviour and cognition, has brought to light of their unconscious interiority exceeds all conscious understanding. It is, in the full sense of the words, transcendent towards consciousness.

Man bears within him the most complex development of unconscious interiority—the result of an evolution of more than three thousand million years. Only on this basis could consciousness unfold. It is by the human unconscious that all conscious activity is nourished, but also limited and guided—on a long lead.

What is communicated (revealed) by inner perception to consciousness—the *subjective* spirit—as command, advice, creative impulse, 'insight' into meaning or understanding, is this unconscious interiority: the *objective* spirit at work in nature. In principle the 'collapse of the metaphysical world' has changed nothing with regard to the nature of the religious *attitude*. It can still be described (as once in the archaic period) as the readiness to be guided by the intentions of a benevolent power which is superior to man (to the Ego). Where the genuineness of the religious attitude is concerned it does not matter whether man imagines this power in heaven or in his own soul. What is crucial is only how far he is capable of hearing its voice and how willing he is to put its directions into practice in his own life. By contrast, however, the mutation of consciousness was not lacking in consequences for forms of religious *behaviour*. Obviously, the 'collapse of the metaphysical world' means that patterns of behaviour which arose out of archaic apperception have become obsolete, and this includes ritual, sacraments and hence the idea of a sacramental ritual fellowship and a consecrated priesthood. At all events the increasing number of people who no longer feel at home in the archaic world-view should be allowed to express their 'religionless religion' as a fully valid form of religious sentiment.

8. THE PASTORAL CARE OF THE INDIFFERENT DEMANDS A STEP FORWARD

Understanding the course of the mutation of consciousness gives us the key to understanding indifference. We can see that as a whole it expresses the fact that people have grown out of the archaic world-view. But we can also see that we must distinguish two groups among the indifferent. First there are those who have fallen prey to the positivist world-view, for although it has been overtaken by evolution, it captured the masses in the last decades. The other group includes those who can sense where this second leap of the mutation has led: they strive to cultivate religious feeling but are unable to do so in the archaic manner. During the first step of the mutation it was a sign of wisdom that the Church was reserved in its attitude to the new; at that time the Church had to guard a deposit to which it alone held the key. Now, however, that the second step has also opened up the religious dimension to those who constitute the advance guard of our time, the Church should not only renounce its reticence but take the opportunity presented to it and risk taking the 'step forward'. For the new world-view is still in the process of development. At the apex of consciousness, which is only now (and with difficulty) emancipating itself from positivism, a struggle is going on. The Church could render a twofold contribution here, in terms of theology and of its spiritual tradition.

For centuries theology has used expressions like 'revelation', 'the living God', 'faith', 'sin', 'redemption', etc., to deal with realities which man experiences in inner perception, realities inaccessible to the positivist sciences. Indeed, depth psychology *has* access, since it is a new type of science with an enlarged empirical concept. As a result of its predominantly pragmatic orientation, however, it is scarcely aware of this yet, and where it *is* aware of it, it must as it were start from scratch. But theology will only be able to make use of the immense start it has if it endeavours to translate into modern thought-patterns its formulations based on archaic apperception.

In terms of how religious feeling is to be *lived*—how man is to be led towards wholeness (salvation)—the Church has a great start in its store of practical experience, acquired above all by the religious orders in their spiritual tradition. Here all the schools of depth psychology will not be able to catch up. But this experience, too, will only be accessible to modern man if it is purified of the dross of the archaic world-view and of a superannuated way of life. If this purification is successful the Church's pastoral care will not need to fear competition from the spiritual traditions of the East or of India, for not only have they developed in the same way against the background of archaic world models, but they have done so with models which are thoroughly alien to Western man.

Translated by Graham Harrison

Heinz Robert Schlette

From Religious Indifference to Agnosticism

RELIGIOUS INDIFFERENCE[1] is not infrequently regarded today as 'modern' and 'normal'. From a philosophical point of view what is involved is a fairly frivolous and superficial attitude. Only if one succeeds in providing an intellectual and existential basis for what can be termed religious indifference can this kind of indifference be interpreted in a way that is of significant interest from the point of view of anthropology and humanism, of politics and public life, of the philosophy of religion and to this extent, too, of Christian theology. All of which is to indicate that the aim of what follows is to examine the distinction between religious indifference and agnosticism in order to try to ease the transition from one to the other.

1. CHARACTERISTICS OF RELIGIOUS INDIFFERENCE

What religious indifference is, is an unavoidable question. But it cannot be answered by introducing some formula to define it. Rather it can only be answered by describing the kind of approach that in general religious indifference is used to denote.[2]

Someone who is not interested in playing chess, looking at modern art, or joining a club can be described as indifferent with regard to these possible activities. But someone who says he rejects chess because he finds it too complicated, because it gives him headaches, or because he does not like the lack of physical exercise, or someone who does not take any pleasure in modern art because he thinks the neglect of representation in favour of abstraction is an intolerable demand, is not in any way to be considered as 'indifferent' with regard to chess or painting. Because of his conscious and deliberate rejection he should rather be seen as very much interested, even if in a negative, not to say polemical, fashion. This gives rise to the question whether the sort of uninterested indifference (if I may be forgiven the pleonasm) that can easily be imagined with regard to chess and other activities exists with regard to such an important question as religion.[3]

Although naturally one very often has the impression, at least in the modern highly developed countries of the First and Second Worlds, that a considerable number of people no longer want to have anything to do with religion (and of course with Christianity and the Church first of all), it would hardly seem to be so easy to provide a statistically satisfactory indication of the extent to which indifference towards religion in fact exists.[4] Instead of starting out from various definitions, impressions, or figures, it strikes me as more useful to bring the problem to life with the help of a handful of admittedly very different examples.

The trial in Jerusalem of Adolf Eichmann, the executant of the Final Solution, revealed his attitude of bureaucratic officialdom for which Hannah Arendt coined the controversial label of the 'banality of evil'. Eichmann's philosophy should be regarded as a cynical perversion of obedience and is characterised by his statement: 'If this thing had to be done'—and he meant the deportation of the Jews—'it was better that calm and order should prevail and that everything should go smoothly.'[5] Perhaps it is possible to talk of indifference in this context to the extent that what is involved is a criminal version of the Stoic virtue of impassivity or *apatheia*. In religious terms Eichmann described himself just before his execution as, in Nazi terminology, a theist.

For a second example I choose the character of Meursault in Camus's early novel *The Outsider* (1942), at least as he is portrayed in the first half of the book: Meursault, insensitive to everything he does and everything that happens to him in the workaday world, whether it is his mother's death or his girlfriend's affection, finally in the noon-day heat kills an Arab on the beach, without feeling intellectually or emotionally involved and above all without any feeling of guilt.[6] This example may be open to the objection that it is purely literary and fictitious. But against this I would insist that in the character of Meursault can very clearly be recognised what in general is meant by uninterested indifference.

A third example is provided by the Austrian writer and philosopher Jean Améry (1912-1978), who after spending several years in Nazi concentration camps lived in Brussels and who on several occasions expounded his attitude to metaphysical and religious questions. In an article with the characteristic title 'Atheism without provocation' he wrote: 'Do I want to know who God is? I am sorry, but I do not. The question is fundamentally not one for me. I find I am in full agreement with Claude Lévi-Strauss . . ., who stated on one occasion: "Personally I am not confronted with the question of God. I find it completely possible to tolerate my life in the knowledge that I shall never be able to explain to myself the totality of the universe." '[7] Does this passage embody the indifference that is not interested in religion? It sounds as if it does, but in Améry's case what is involved is a justified indifference whose background is provided on the one hand by the claims of the Viennese Circle's logical positivism and on the other what he experienced in the surroundings of Austrian popular Catholicism and later in Nazi concentration camps.[8]

One could therefore ask again, more urgently: Does the attitude and mentality of lack of interest that is called indifference really exist? From the religious point of view are not those who are called indifferent rather those who are disillusioned or resigned, those who have despaired, those who have been hurt by religion and the world of religion? And must one not see, too, that among the apparently indifferent are those who are only partially indifferent: to Christianity, say, but not to Buddhism; to institutional Christianity (the Church), but not to Jesus; to religion as a compendium of definite truths of salvation, rituals, moral precepts, etc., but not to the function that religion automatically performs socially and politically, even independent of its own religious content?[9] Clearly it is in practice impossible to produce any general formulation in view of the multiplicity of different forms in which religious indifference appears and in view of the variety of ultimately undiscoverable motives, experiences, attitudes, and injuries that are hidden behind what appears or parades itself as indifference. But it is the lot of philosophy to want to make general statements despite all the difficulties of detail, and hence in our context, too, it is impossible to avoid talking of religious indifference with a certain degree of generalisation and abstraction. But what cannot be disputed is the danger of using the inevitability of abstraction as an excuse for talking about a phantom that does not exist in reality.

To avoid any misunderstanding, I cannot and do not want to assert that people who are in fact indifferent to religion do not exist at all. My view is simply that those who allegedly are indifferent to religion often suffer from damage and disappointment caused by religion itself; that often what we have to deal with is partial religious indifference; and that, notwithstanding the difficulties of describing and characterising religious indifference exactly, it is not without meaning and justification to give a certain play to the generalised image of complete religious indifference as an intellectual construct in order to put to it, despite the unavoidable abstraction, the questions and introduce the reflections that suggest themselves, as long as one does not oneself become indifferent with regard to religious indifference by failing any longer to question, reflect on and criticise it.

2. AGNOSTICISM IN DISTINCTION TO RELIGIOUS INDIFFERENCE

At the level of generality and abstraction that is proper to it philosophy has for a long time been discussing the problems of religious indifference. It has done so under the headings of scepticism and agnosticism, though with a characteristic distinction between these terms that we shall now discuss.

When something like religious indifference actually began to exist is a question which, if only because of the necessary nuances I have indicated, is historically not easy to answer and need not be gone into here. Nevertheless it is worth recalling that the articulation of scepticism in questions of metaphysics and religion goes back a very long way, even if it is only since the nineteenth century that this kind of scepticism has been labelled agnosticism.[10] Without, therefore, wanting to insert a historical excursus I should simply like to mention that fragment B 4 of the sophist Protagoras can be regarded as one of the earliest pieces of evidence for scepticism with regard to metaphysics and religion and in this sense for agnosticism: 'Of the Gods I have no knowledge—neither that they exist, nor that they do not exist, nor what kind of form they have. For there is much that impedes this kind of knowledge—the obscurity of the question at issue and the brevity of human life.'[11] But—and this is the point of this brief historical interlude—would it not be wrong to label Protagoras and those who thought like him as indifferent to religion? Is it not precisely the opposite of indifference that is the reason for Protagoras speaking as he does?

Hence precisely if one accepts that scepticism and agnosticism *can* give rise to religious indifference as the attitude in the living of one's life of a complete lack of interest in everything concerned with religion (just as atheism can naturally also give rise to indifference, even if atheism as a negation of religion is fundamentally interested in religion), one obviously and correctly starts from the assumption that indifference and agnosticism are in no way identical. At all events it can be said that, as often happens, what is termed practical agnosticism can be equated with religious indifference to the extent that it represents an attitude of habitual lack of interest. Even if one rejects the term practical agnosticism because it is open to misunderstanding, the essential difference between indifference and agnosticism becomes clearly recognisable: religious indifference in the precise and strict sense does not reflect upon itself, since if it were to do so it would emerge from its state of lack of interest by trying to comprehend and justify itself as this lack of interest, and precisely by means of this act of self-reflection religious indifference would turn into religious scepticism or agnosticism. The distinction, or at least one extremely important distinction, lies in the fact that agnosticism is aware of itself as an attitude based on reflection or philosophical proof, while religious indifference does not even reflect on itself (which would presuppose a no longer indifferent interest in perception and truth) but merely dismisses religion with a shrug of the shoulders.

This kind of contrast between religious indifference on the one hand and agnosticism or religious scepticism on the other does no doubt present rather an ideal pattern, since at this level the situations of actual life are infinitely varied. The question can thus be raised whether to think in this ideal generalising way of indifference and agnosticism as sharply distinct from each other is not far too abstract and too remote from the world. That this is not the case and that it is rather the reverse, that this distinction was only drawn to indicate some connections of great importance in the fields of anthropology and humanism, of politics and public life, and indeed of religion too, must and, I hope, will emerge from what follows.

3. FROM RELIGIOUS INDIFFERENCE TO AGNOSTICISM

If one imagines how the attitude of someone who is indifferent to things in general and especially to religion would present itself in actual daily life, what emerges is the once again ideal and generalised picture of a nihilism which is theoretically suffused by boredom although perhaps extremely active, which is not aware of itself and hence does not also comprehend the affirmative implications that it has continually created and accomplished by the mere fact of carrying on and going on living. In this bored, unthinking, unconscious nihilism (that is, a nihilism that is not aware of itself) which only continues in a purely natural way, I see a mode of human existence which must be labelled deficient. No doubt this a clear value judgment. I introduce it consciously and deliberately, even if I am quite clear about the difficulties that are linked with it and also with the fact that it is not possible here to enter in more detail into the problems of how and whether this value judgment can be justified. But anyone who agrees with the conclusion that religious indifference is a deficient mode of life must raise the question whether and how it is possible to overcome it.

This question lands one in a paradox. On the basis of the description of religious indifference in the various forms in which it occurs we have typified it as unreflective, unconscious, bored, uninterested—well aware that actual examples never correspond completely to these ideal patterns. But how can it ever be possible to overcome this kind of attitude since quite clearly those conditions are lacking that are needed for it to be overcome—the desire for knowledge, for the truth, for commitment, etc? It looks as if one is trying to square the circle.

In reality one should at once abandon efforts to overcome indifference were it not that one had to reckon with the fact that in practice religious indifference does not appear in its pure form, that in fact it signifies a deficiency, and thus a lack and a weakness, and that most probably it is not completely impossible and hopeless to address it in the expectation of nevertheless being able to liberate it from its bored nihilism or its nihilistic ennui.

I have deliberately used the circumlocution 'most probably . . . not completely impossible and hopeless' in order to express my preference for an attempt at dialogue that would be both critical and realistic, both sceptical and psychological. With this approach I would hope to avoid a method and way of thought often to be met with among traditional and what are termed Christian philosophers: the form of argument that for a variety of reasons is in agreement in presupposing that there is to be found in man's essential nature an *a priori* fundamental orientation which may be termed transcendental, natural, innate, or something similar (or described in Aristotelian and Thomist terms like an arrow speeding to its mark) and which inevitably compels him towards the transcendent, the divine, 'God', or 'the absolute'. Although it is admitted that for historical, psychological, sociological or similar reasons this fundamental orientation can in particular cases be distorted or swamped to the point where it can no longer be recognised, nevertheless at the same time it is claimed that it can never be completely lacking.

If on the basis of this well-known theory which I do not need to discuss in greater detail here, a theory which can indeed be described as classic, one tries to engage in argument with religious indifference, in my view a series of objective and psychological difficulties arise. One will doubtless tend to give a negative interpretation to religious indifference's lack of awareness and its deficiency on the basis of one's own 'knowledge' of man's essential *a priori* determination. Linked occasionally (and also unintentionally) with this knowledge is an attitude of superiority which is experienced by the indifferent as an arrogant knowing better or as a condescending shrug of the shoulders and in any case is viewed with suspicion. Quite apart from the insinuation of moral weakness in the sense of the entry mentioned above: 'Indifference, religious, see Inertia, spiritual',[12] the person who is religiously indifferent will at once get the impression that he or she cannot converse with this partner on the same level, in other words on the human level. Rather, in the person who objects to his or her indifference and wants to overcome it he or she will sense a self-proclaimed superior being with special élitist and gnostic insights with whom he or she cannot share the common human task of questioning and searching.

Now, I do not want to, and I cannot, assert that this classic theory is completely untrue and that necessarily it is always impossible to start the dialogue with religious indifference on this kind of basis. My point is simply that the difficulties I have mentioned do in fact exist, as of course do others, especially in view of the contemporary philosophical justification of the classic theory; and for this reason I prefer a different approach to religious indifference. This method may itself continue to be marked by the conviction of the old approach about man's essential nature and his essential orientation to the absolute (something that for the sake of honesty should not be kept silent about); it may in addition remain 'unsuccessful' or ultimately produce less than one may have expected; but, along with all the objections one can bring against it, it seems to me to have the advantage of greater existential solidarity with religious indifference and hence also the advantage of greater credibility.

In order, therefore, for the overcoming—or, better, the transcending—of religious indifference to succeed, what is needed, according to the realistic and sceptical starting-point chosen here, is to betake oneself to the point where religious indifference itself finds itself and where therefore the chance is greatest of encouraging it to a certain extent to accompany one. If in this kind of rapprochement one refrains from efforts at apologetics in favour of religion or indeed Christianity and merely tries to bring religious indifference to an awareness of itself or of its own ideas, it is theoretically possible that the transition from this indifference to agnosticism will be recognised as legitimate without anything like a 'religious trap' being suspected.

Hence the transition to agnosticism can only happen, if at all, if religious indifference does not experience itself as being under external attack or indeed put under any pressure (for example by being exposed to certain personal affirmations, experiences, insights, sacred texts, authoritative statements, the threat of eternal punishment, and this kind of thing). It can only happen if religious indifference feels itself to be genuinely accepted and understood by a partner which is able to locate its starting-point in human solidarity. This partner, however, can only be philosophy, because this alone is in the situation of being able methodically to share the deficiency of indifference and, without religious or missionary ulterior motives, to lead it over to the level of thought of agnosticism. In this one can see a service that in its way, and on its own (rational and humane) level, philosophy is able to do for the benefit of genuine humanity.

Perhaps many will regard this transition from indifference to agnosticism as too short a step and too insignificant and will be disappointed that there is not talk here of a form of overcoming indifference which, on the basis of the classic theory I have papaphrased, would lead abruptly to a religious or even the Christian position. To the extent that this objection does not arise from illusions about the possibility of justifying the approach to religion (and Christianity) on the basis of contemporary philosophy, or from an all too fashionable interest (and at the same time one that has its commercial possibilities) in religious renewal or even renaissance, one must accept that it expresses a widespread lack of understanding for, and uneasiness with, agnosticism.

This prejudice linked with ignorance is particulary rife in Catholicism, it has to be said clearly. The main reason for this is the way this term has become taboo as a result of what Vatican I had to say about what is termed natural theology or the possibility of 'proving' the existence of God and as a result of the condemnation of modernism.[13] This taboo led to the narrowing down of the question of agnosticism to the question of the viability of metaphysics, and this in turn led to the various philosophical dimensions of this subject being hardly considered seriously in Catholic circles—quite differently from what happened in Protestant circles.

4. THE PERSPECTIVES OF AGNOSTICISM

The deep-rooted prejudice and sheer ignorance that occur in connection with agnosticism can admittedly only be countered by a patient process of enlightenment and education. Without being able to fulfil this programme here I shall simply try to sketch the extent to which, in my view, agnosticism represents a stance which it is as important as it is topical to investigate more precisely. I shall limit myself to expounding three sets of problems that have already been mentioned.

As far as philosophy's understanding of man and the humanism that corresponds to this are concerned, agnosticism reveals the insight that religious indifference ultimately finds its justification in human inability to provide by means of philosophy a definitive answer to the old question of where we come from, where we are going to, and what it is all for, in other words the question of what human life means. If I am right in accepting this thesis, then it means that all images of mankind are false that give the impression of being able or claim to be able to provide a very good answer to this question on the basis of philosophy alone. The reverse is true, that philosophical anthropology and humanism must understand themselves as 'open' or in other words as not being fixed and determined or being capable of being fixed and determined, in either a positive or a negative sense, as far as metaphysics and religion are concerned.

From this kind of openness there follows, at the social and political level, the possibility of a critique of ideology[14] over against all those who, whatever their methods and reasons, claim to have found the philosopher's stone. This fundamental distance from ideologies as philosophically unverifiable sets of assertions then gives rise, in the sphere of practical philosophy and how people actually live, to the demand for mutual respect, toleration, awareness of one's own limitations, a readiness to understand the other person's point of view: indeed, on this basis one could easily develop a whole philosophy of peace. At this level religion and the religions are of course addressed, to the extent that it becomes clear that no religion has, in terms of philosophy, left agnosticism behind or is able to do so and that instead every religion necessarily rests on specific options and insights that cannot be proved philosophically and therefore cannot be turned into absolute general postulates.

This already indicates that particularly with regard to the philosophy of religion agnosticism is fitted to make us aware of the way religion has a particular context or, as I would prefer to put it, of religion's gnoseological status. Religion always rests on options, agreements, decisions, etc., that transcend the boundaries of what can be known by philosophy. This awareness, which is not fundamentally anything surprising or sensational, naturally includes the possibility of agnosticism as the reflex form of religious indifference leading with good reasons to a non-religious or anti-religious option, whether this be in favour of atheism or of a secularised philosophy of life.

This also shows that moving from religious indifference to an agnosticism that is aware of itself is also always a transition from an unaware and nihilistically uninterested fatalism to the consciously apprehended freedom of the active agent.[15] It must be clearly recognised that this freedom includes the agnostic's ability to refuse to plump for any particular option so as to remain at the level of agnosticism in complete rational and philosophical clarity. This attitude should not be damned from the Christian point of view with reference to Rev. 3:16, where the community of Laodicea is warned to be either cold or hot but not lukewarm. This text is completely out of place here because an agnosticism that remains itself represents a stance of extreme sensibility and watchfulness which has nothing to do with tepidity or lukewarmness.

As recent research has shown, it is desirable to distinguish between definite variants and nuances within agnosticism.[16] This question cannot be gone into here, but I would merely like to point out that one should distinguish a pre-religious and a post-religious agnosticism. While the former does not close itself off against the possibility of making a choice, the latter seems to regard itself as representing a final stage of reflection when options are no longer open. An obvious supposition is that religious indifference is most often aware of itself as a post-religious agnosticism, though this must not be seen as a necessary conclusion.

In general it should be emphasised once again that we are not of the opinion that the actual multiplicity of living situations can be pinned down in terse abstractions and formal definitions. Hence our investigations did not have the primary object of developing a particular method of dialogue or indeed of providing pastoral or educational hints and similar advice. Rather it has been a question primarily of a philosophical exposition of the gnoseological status of religion, ideology, philosophy of life, etc. Even if the freedom that on this basis is to be acknowledged as belonging to agnosticism in fact does not and indeed cannot exist in most actual situations, because people's minds are already made up on the basis of tradition, environment, education, etc., and they do not live in the abstraction of this freedom, nevertheless it is of considerable practical value to recognise this gnoseological status as such in order to understand the reality and possibility of human and humanist solidarity as well as the quality and extent of the divisions and differences that exist between people.

In conclusion it is worth mentioning that the philosophical agnosticism recommended as superior to the deficiencies of religious indifference should be of interest to theology not only because it clearly admits of an option in favour of Christian faith (an option the detailed working out and justification of which would be the job of fundamental theology), but because here there comes into play a mode of philosophical thought which, explicitly or not, is largely dominant today and as 'philosophy' can look to the kind of attention on the part of theology that was earlier bestowed on other philosophies. From this point of view special attention should be paid to the fact that recently Karl Rahner has explicitly expounded the importance of agnosticism for theology.[17]

Rahner rejects the stance of 'philistine indifference' which 'does not bother itself at all about the incomprehensibility and unmanageability of our existence'. On the other hand he recognises as theology's partner in discussion that agnosticism 'which forms part of our ultimate experience and is really the burning pain of our existence'. In conscious agnosticism Ranher sees a contemporary expression of what theology has taught as the incomprehensibility of God. Hence in his view one must recognise that in this sense agnosticism is a necessary aspect of Christian faith itself. Rahner ends by

E

saying: 'The agnosticism of the philistines and of the self-important philosophers is only the failed attempt of the true agnosticism that is demanded of the Christian. For the latter worships in hope and love the incomprehensibility that is called God, and in this occurs his or her faith.' Whatever may be said about this theological interpretation of agnosticism, it certainly represents a powerful stimulus to thought and needs to be reproduced here as such—not least with special respect for Karl Rahner, from whom we always have something to learn.

Translated by Robert Nowell

Notes

1. While the German terms *Indifferenz* and *Gleichgültigkeit* can be used synonymously in the negative sense that is intended here, both can also denote the philosophical or mystical attitude of spiritual repose and calm: see K. Nusser, s.v. *Gleichgültigkeit*, in *Historisches Wörterbuch der Philosophie* ed. J. Ritter (Basle/Stuttgart 1974) III col. 671. It is noteworthy that in the third edition of *Die Religion in Geschichte und Gegenwart* (Tübingen 1956 ff.) neither *Gleichgültigkeit* nor *Indifferenz* (or *Indifferentismus*) is treated under a separate heading, while the second edition of the *Lexicon für Theologie und Kirche* (Freiburg 1957 ff.) has a short article on *Indifferentismus* by K. Algermissen (vol. V cols. 651-652, with useful bibliography), while vol. IV col. 958, dating from 1960, has under *Gleichgültigkeit* (indifference) simply a cross-reference to *Trägheit, geistige* (spiritual inertia).

2. To be precise, religious indifference is of course non-religious, but I would sooner not be bothered with such pedantry.

3. In what follows I am using the term religion in its colloquial and rather imprecise sense. On the complicated problem of formulating a concept of religion see my entry on 'Religion' in *Handbuch philosophischer Grundbegriffe* eds. H. Krings, H. M. Baumgartner and C. Wild (Munich 1974) pp. 1233-1250.

4. According to the statistics in the *World Christian Encyclopedia*, Comparative Survey of Churches and Religions in the Modern World, ed. D. Barrett (Oxford 1982), a fifth of the world's population of 4,200 million is without religion, but what this means for the extent of religious indifference is hardly clear. See G. Mack in *Die Zeit*, 13 August 1982, p. 37.

5. See H. Arendt *Eichmann in Jerusalem. Ein Bericht von der Banalität des Bösen* (1964) pp. 232 and 300 of the 1978 paperback edition (Reinbek).

6. A. Camus *L'Etranger* in A. Camus *Théatre, Récits, Nouvelles* (Paris 1962) pp. 1125-1166. See also the very interesting study by C. Treil *L'Indifférence dans l'oeuvre d'Albert Camus* (Montreal 1971), which in general offers important distinctions within the concept of indifference: see pp. 15-23.

7. In J. Améry *Widersprüche* (Stuttgart 1971) p. 23.

8. See J. Améry 'Das Jahrhundert ohne Gott' in *Die Zukunft der Philosophie* ed. H. R. Schlette (Olten/Freiburg 1968) pp. 13-33, and see also his *Jenseits von Schuld und Sühne. Bewältigungsversuch eines Überwältigten* (Munich 1966).

9. On this, see N. Luhmann *Funktion der Religion* (Frankfurt 1977) and H. Lübbe 'Religion nach der Aufklärung' in H. Lübbe *Philosophie nach der Aufklärung. Von der Notwendigkeit pragmatischer Vernunft* (Düsseldorf/Vienna 1980) pp. 59-85.

10. Apart from the appropriate entries in encyclopaedias, particularly that in *The Encyclopedia of Philosophy* ed. P. Edwards (New York/London 1967), eight vols., I shall confine myself to citing C. Wild *Philosophische Skepsis* (Königstein 1980); K.-D. Ulke *Agnostisches im Viktorianischen England* (Freiburg/Munich 1980); and *Der moderne Agnostizismus* ed. H. R. Schlette (Düsseldorf 1979).

11. I quote the translation by W. Bröcker *Die Geschichte der Philosophie vor Sokrates* (Frankfurt 1965) p. 113.

12. See note 1 above.

13. See H. R. Schlette 'Vom Atheismus zum Agnostizismus' in *Der moderne Agnostizismus* ed. H. R. Schlette (Düsseldorf 1979) pp. 214-216; K.-H. Weger *Der Mensch vor dem Anspruch Gottes. Glaubensbegründung in einer agnostischen Welt* (Graz/Vienna/Cologne 1981) pp. 203-218.

14. See H. R. Schlette 'Aporetik—Kriteriologie—philosophische Ideologiekritik' in *Die Zukunft der Philosophie* ed. H. R. Schlette (Olten/Freiburg 1968) pp. 184-202.

15. It would be worth while reflecting specifically on the connection between agnosticism, human dignity and human rights.

16. See the individual essays in *Der moderne Agnostizismus* ed. H. R. Schlette (Düsseldorf 1979), and see also A. J. Buch 'Begrenztes Problemdenken. Zur Ausschaltung der Gottesfrage in der Metaphysik' in *Nicolai Hartmann 1882-1982* ed. A. J. Buch (Bonn 1982) pp. 97-122. There is also the extremely stimulating study by B.-U. Hergemöller *Weder—Noch. Traktat über die Sinnfrage* (Münster 1982), which at the moment is only in typescript.

17. See K. Rahner 'Der bennende Schmerz unserer Existenz. Glaubensbegründung in einer agnostischen Welt' in *Frankfurter Allgemeine Zeitung* (10 April 1982), *Bilder und Zeiten* supplement.

Claude Geffré

The Outlook for the Christian Faith in a World of Religious Indifference

IT WAS Dietrich Bonhoeffer who asked the question: 'What should we do to make Christ become Lord of the irreligious?' This is much the same question as the one this article sets out to tackle, since my task is to reflect on how the Christian faith should present itself in the context of a world indifferent to religion.

Several previous contributions have diagnosed what is meant by 'religious indifference', so there is no need to do so again here, but it is worth remarking that one should perhaps be wary of using the term too readily of the Western world. My purpose is to study the problem posed to Christians by the massive evidence of indifference to religion. Here we are talking about a state of affairs permitted by God. Now the question of God can no longer be posed by anyone anywhere, but rather than plunge into a theology of lamentation for this fact, we need to face up clearly to the actual situation and ask ourselves if it does not affect the type of faith we are used to, if it does not present us with a radical challenge in regard to the God to whom we appeal. As has often happened in the history of Christianity, what might at first seem to be a menace threatening the very future of faith, later turns out to have been a liberating factor.

I will start by recalling the complexity of the phenomenon of religious indifference in the world of today, then go on to ask what should be the dominant note of a Christian faith lived amidst indifference. Finally, I shall ask what might be the face of God in a cultural context of an absent God.

1. THE LOW EBB OF RELIGION

There is no denying that today we are witnessing an indifference to religion on a massive scale, at least in the Northern Hemisphere, in Europe and North America. Some people may talk about a 'return of religion', but there is no turning the clock back beyond the atheistic critique of religion, beginning in the eighteenth century. As far as the masses are concerned, it would be truer to speak of a sort of spiritual daze in the sense that the question of God simply no longer arises. What is most surprising is the fact that religious faith somehow still goes on. But the non-relevance of God is simply accepted as a *normal* state of affairs, something fully consonant with what modern man sees as reasonable.

(a) In trying to analyse the phenomenon of religious indifference, it is not enough merely to invoke the modern process of *secularisation*; it needs to be linked also to the *present crisis of ideologies*. In some Western countries, such as France, the great cultural change of the past fifteen years has been the failure of Marxism as an ideology, caused principally by the manifest failure of the socialist countries to fulfil their claims to embody the communist ideal. Indifference to the Christian faith is only one aspect of a more generalised indifference to the theoretical programmes of various humanisms— classic liberal democracy as well as Marxist humanism. The practical religious indifference of the great majority is consistent with a culture deeply marked by *nihilism*. This is why one can speak of a 'post-atheistic' indifference.

This nihilism is linked to the success of the social sciences and their anti-humanist trend. Certain Western intellectual circles are much closer to Nietzsche than to Marx. If 'God is dead', man has not taken his place. What we are left with is the earth and the 'world game', as Nietzsche called it. As Michel Foucault has written: 'What Nietzsche's thought proclaims is not so much the death of God as the death of his murderer, man.' Now, thanks to the explosion of culture and the rapid spread of ideas, contemporary mankind is not only lacking God, but lacking man as well. Religious indifference is both the effect and the symptom of a more general crisis of *meaning* which is striking hard at religions and ideologies with their claim to provide a final explanation of the destiny of mankind and the course of history. There is no doubt that the claims of all humanisms have been exposed by man's tragic fate over the past quarter-century.

(b) There is a definite link between religious indifference and the crisis of ideologies. But paradoxically, this crisis can also explain the 'return of religion' referred to so complacently over the past few years. Turning back to God can indeed work as a response to the disenchantment stemming from the crisis of ideologies and the spiritual void left by a world dominated by technical reasoning.

The crisis of ideologies, however, is not the only factor; there is also the bankruptcy of *temporal religions* which refuse God in the name of the messianic value of history. Against this, there is a return to religions of transcendance such as Islam, and the revolt is made in the name of faith. So we could be witnessing a surpising inversion of what has, since Feuerbach, been an accepted slogan of modern atheistic humanism, namely that God and human freedom are incompatible. Whereas once the existence of God underwrote the established order and made any human revolt impossible, now it is the major inspiration of struggles for human liberation. It looks as though we might be on the threshold of a new age in which God has to come to the help of a humanity which is beginning to doubt its demiurgic power. But one has to see the ambiguity inherent in this critique of modern thought by a newly triumphant religion; as the tragic case of Iran shows, it can lead to a divinisation of politics and so to the most primitive forms of theocratism and intolerance. And this collusion between religion and political power can lead to a reaction producing a new and deep religious indifference, even though the reasons behind it are quite different from those generally obtaining in a culture dominated by technical rationalism.

(c) In any case, it is difficult to make a simple judgment on religious indifference. Nearly forty years after Bonhoeffer, one cannot simply echo his diagnosis that modern man is completely irreligious. Against those—including Christians—who have become the protagonists of secularisation, one has to note that religion is not necessarily the expression of a series of social and economic alienations. Neither does it have to be the expression of a lack, an insecurity or a primeval *angst*. Bonhoeffer was right to point to the maturity and autonomy of modern man and his consequent intolerance of an alienating religion. But his verdict on religion as always synonymous with religiosity, alienation or evasion was too pessimistic. In particular, he was too quick to attribute the irreligion of modern man to the secularisation of our Western societies and the waning of the influence of the Christian churches. It is true that in the countries that make up the old Christendom, many people are no longer Christian, but this does not mean that they have become completely irreligious. We Christians are too quick to judge the religious situation of Western man as though the Church had a monopoly of the sacred.

More fundamentally, one can ask if Bonhoeffer did not exaggerate the 'faith-religion' dichotomy which is a heritage of reformed theology. Today we are more alert to the apologetic exploitation of this distinction made in certain Catholic circles. This has abstracted the Christian *faith* from the basic challenge of atheism, as though Christianity were not itself a religion, while trying also to provide an ideological justification for the religious indifference of our contemporaries. One might in fact ask whether the assurance with which we proclaim the lack of a religious *a priori* in modern man is not a way of reassuring ourselves in the face of the failure of the Church's mission.

So one should not be too quick to speak of religion having reached its lowest ebb in our contemporaries. The distinction between 'faith' and 'unbelief' is certainly too narrow to take account of all the cases in between. We need three terms: faith, beliefs, unbelief. We are witnessing an increase in irrational beliefs and God is reappearing where we did not expect him, outside the official churches. But even when we pass a more optimistic verdict on the religious feelings or sense of the sacred of our contemporaries, this does not mean that we have to go back on our general diagnosis of the deep indifference shown by our societies to official religions. A sympathetic approach to various manifestations of the sacred can well go hand in hand with complete indifference to the message and forms of historical Christianity. We now need to reflect on what form Christianity ought to take in the face of this indifference.

2. THE NATURE OF A POST-ATHEIST FAITH

Much—too much—has been made of the 'purifying' role of atheism. I would rather not speculate on the providential function of indifference. . . . But it is one thing to decide whether the fate of faith is a 'good thing' or a 'bad thing', and another to try to think *theologically* about what happens to the faith that belongs to all ages in a climate of religious indifference. I will limit myself to four main points.

(a) The critical test for faith

Faith lived in a climate of religious indifference is necessarily subject to a *critical testing*. In the term used as the title of a French book published some years ago, it is always an 'exposed faith'.[1] The object of faith does not change, and there is a unity of faith throughout the ages in its properly theologal goals. But in so far as faith is rooted in a historically conditioned human subjectivity there is a *history of faith* just as there is a history of the question of the existence of God. As Paul Ricoeur put it, 'what is available for belief' by man changes. By 'what is available for belief' (*'croyable disponible'*) he meant the structures of credibility or plausibility which form the conscience of believers at a particular time.

If faith today is going through a critical test, this is not just because of the traditional critique of religion as formulated by Feuerbach, nor only because of the 'deconstructive' work of those masters of suspicion Nietzsche, Marx and Freud. On a more general level and a practical rather than theoretical one, religious indifference is the result of the lack of relevance of a particular historical form of Christianity to the basic questions modern man is asking about the future of the world. There is nothing new in what one believes no longer coinciding with what one knows. This is where the process that began with the Enlightenment as human emancipation and a conflict between the authority of reason and the authority of faith finally leads. But today many people in whom the new image of the world and of mankind resulting from the progress made by the natural and social sciences is deeply ingrained feel the divorce between new *states of consciousness* and the traditional statements of the Christian faith most acutely.

Faced with this new outlook of indifference, faith can no longer afford to be a naïve faith. One can speak of a 'second naïvety', resulting precisely from the critical testing to which faith is subjected now: we need to keep the word 'naïvety' in order to stress that all this work of critical examination does not compromise the *spontaneity* of faith. The nature of the faith required in a context of religious indifference is that of reciprocal interaction between the critical demands of an intelligence sharpened by modern suspicion and the 'obedience of faith' in the sense meant by St Paul.

(b) The hermeneutical instantiation of faith

There can be no critical faith subjected to the test of religious indifference without a *certain reinterpretation of Christianity*. Let us say that Christian faith today necessarily involves a hermeneutical instantiation. Bonhoeffer essayed a 'non-religious' interpretation of Christianity. One can well ask what form transmission of the Christian message might take for men with no religious background and no expectation of personal salvation.

This hermeneutical operation would start from a critical analysis of the world as we experience it today; it would try to rediscover the basic elements of the Christian experience as witnessed by the New Testament and seek to establish a critical correlation between the world of our experience today and that basic Christian experience described in the New Testament.[2] To state here that there is no experience of faith without a hermeneutical experience is just another way of saying that there can be no living faith without theology, at least in the general sense of a confrontation with a particular culture.

Talking of an interpretative instantiation within faith means taking seriously both the historicity of truth, including revealed truth, and the historicity of the believer. There can in fact be no act of faith that does not also involve an act of interpreting the world. The Christian faith depends essentially on an origin, Jesus Christ, its founding event. But I cannot get back to that origin except through the New Testament witness, overlaid with all the historical depth of a believing community subject to the need to legitimise, to identify. The experience of the early Christian community is normative for the Church for all time, but there is an *analogy* between the New Testament and the part it played in the early Christian community and the part played by that community in a historically conditioned Church.[3]

In other words, true tradition does not consist of mechanical repetition of a chemically pure *corpus* of doctrine; it is rather, with the guarantee of the gift of the Spirit, a creative reinterpretation, a will to bring new historical embodiments of Christianity into being, both in the realm of confession of faith and in that of practice. Today, our situation of religious indifference summons us to a radical questioning of the identity of Christianity. Many Christians are tired of endless intra-church debates, in which the progressives are as passionately wrapped up as the traditionalists. They feel that the *real debate* lies elsewhere. If they have the courage to follow their intuition to its logical conclusion, they have to admit that their faith has become *unreal*, and that this unreality stems precisely from their efforts to be honest with their actual experience, with the echo of the contemporary world and its questions sounding within themselves. Today people no longer live with the messianic expectation they held when the Christian message was first preached. They now feel a mixture of unshakeable hope for a humanly viable future and terror caused by the fact that the nuclear threat hangs, for the first time, over the whole of humanity. This is the background against which we must reinterpret Christianity and make the Christian message relevant.

(c) The co-existence of faith and unbelief

Unlike the state of affairs that obtained when the Christian religion was part of the cultural language of everyone, the faith of believers is no longer protected by its sociological environment. It is a delicate plant shaken by every breeze, smothered by the luxuriant crops of a culture further and further removed from the great statements of faith. But the opportunity of such a faith—outside any religious context—is to recover its true nature of free gift of God and free act of man.

Faith is going to feel the effects of this freedom and share in the *insecurity* which characterises personal freedom. After religion as content and security has crumbled away, the leap of faith is going to shine out as 'opting for the impossible'. It will be a risky bet, in the sense that it will no longer be a definite possession, a closed certainty, once acquired never let go. I may question many of the statements in the *Credo*; no matter, provided I keep this basic attitude of receiving the meaning of my life and of the world from a Word of which I am neither the author nor the master. The risk a post-atheist faith runs is that of being lived in constant insecurity; but the chance it has is that of finally ceasing to be unreal. 'The place of faith is in reality, since the extreme decision I have had to take has made me be the subject of my faith in reality and not somewhere else (which means both nowhere and in an unrealised part of reality). Being present to reality is then no longer a second step, but the initial act by which believing takes on meaning and results in action.'[4]

A faith returned to its true nature is also a faith returned to its proper *obscurity*. For centuries, the Christian faith coincided with the structures of plausibility of Western society. But 'what is available for belief' to modern man has changed; that is, the discontinuity between the world of the truths of faith and that of the verifiable realities of our experience is felt far more acutely. This is true to the extent that many people must wonder if we are not being driven back to *fideism*.

Faith does not have to be fideist just because it can no longer base itself on the traditional religious supports. It has to show its own intelligibility within itself, without any trace of extrinsic credibility preceding the act of faith. Faith is always an opening to a meaning that comes to me, which is given to me from somewhere else. But the inner evidence proper to faith only comes to the surface at the secret point where the freedom of my love meets the free gift of God. Outside this free exchange of human and divine wills, faith can always be suspected of being an absurd wager or simply the projection of my all-powerful desires.

This leads one to conclude that there is a sort of *existential co-existence* of faith and unbelief in every believer.[5] While a theologian like St Thomas Aquinas held that *doubt* was sinful in itself, we should see doubt as an intrinsic, and even positive, element of faith lived in a climate of indifference. 'Difficulty' would perhaps be too strong a term; 'doubt' is better, provided one does not take it in the moral sense used in classical theology.

(d) God is absent for everyone

To finish defining the nature of the faith needed to survive a context of religious indifference, I should like to pose the idea of a special brotherhood of believers and unbelievers, *facing the same fate of the absence of God in the world*.

Here one can take up Bonhoeffer's insight when he warned us that the believer today has to take on the truth of human existence in the world as though God did not exist, '*etsi*

Deus non daretur', as St Anselm said before him. The paradox of this spiritual experience consists in living God's absence *before God*. If one omits the *'coram Deo'*, in the strong sense used by Luther, the paradox dissolves. But if we go on living Christianity as a religion designed to make up for man's incapacity or to compensate for his inadequacy, we are not taking the crisis of religion seriously. I have to live my prayerful submission to God even though every day, in my life and in the world, I sense its uselessness. This is why the believer need not feel any complex in comparison with the unbeliever so far as human authenticity goes; he is just as much alone in shouldering his burden as a human being.

So our historical situation of religious indifference calls us to demystify the concept of faith that would confuse it with the utilitarian, security-giving function of religion. I would add that it calls us equally to demystify that concept of faith which is confused with the still primeval quest for an infallible truth. We all certainly still feel nostalgia for an origin identified with the fullness of truth, and as a result of this dream, too, of a body of doctrine capable of being an adequate translation of that truth. In other words, we are not willing to live our faith in a permanent search, stumbling as we go, in non-response to all our questions. This is why some people have seen a 'pathology of truth' as part of a type of intransigent Catholicism.

As a conclusion to this attempt to sketch a typology of faith lived in a context of indifference, I should just like to recall that Revelation should not be understood purely as a reply to our questions. Revelation is also the history of man's questioning of God. And this history of man's questioning of God can teach us as much about faith as Revelation understood purely as a reply to man's questions. If the future for our Western societies is one of religious indifference, this at least has the advantage of making us understand that seeing man as God's affair and God as a reply to man's questioning is an outrageous simplification of the terms of the religious problem.

3. A GOD MARKED BY GRATUITOUSNESS

Having tried to define the nature of faith in a context of religious indifference, we now need to examine the *theological* significance of that indifference, what it means for our understanding of God. A faith lived without religious foundations contradicts any sort of utilitarian God. We have to experience God as marked by gratuitousness.

The movement of secularisation which has been going on since the Enlightenment has meant that religion has progressively withdrawn from every sphere in which man has acquired knowledge and therefore mastery. If we take Feuerbach's classic view, we will conclude that the spread of religion belongs to a still infantile stage of human development and that the new maturity of modern man must therefore coincide with the end of religion as human alienation and shedding of responsibility. As long as man was not fully himself, while he alienated his own substance in the absolute, God performed a certain number of functions in human life and in the world. We might say that God withdraws as man's power advances.

As E. Jüngel has said, we must exploit the modern discovery of the 'wordly non-necessity' of God in a genuinely theological way.[6] Man can be human without God, and the world is interesting in itself without any reference to God. Stating the non-necessity of God in a world in which mankind has come of age leads us to discover that utilitarian versions of God are no longer relevant.

(a) Critique of utilitarian versions of God

(i) The first version to be called into question is the God of *metaphysical theism*, which operates in terms of beginning and end and as such functions in utilitarian categories. 'Such a system, whatever its historical embodiments, can be exactly defined. It is guided throughout by utility, by calculation. By giving oneself a fixed point, one in fact sets up an ideally designed model and sets out to imitate it. So we give ourselves a picture of the world. Whether in archaeology or teleology, the image is always the same.'[7] The God of the Alliance supervenes outside the register of our images and our interests. He exists in the order of gratuitous gift, gift with no reason, the unknown that cuts across our lives, the wound of our desire.

This leads us to question, too, the Omnipotence and Lordship of God. From the viewpoint of the necessity of God in the world, his Lordship is seen as absolute and jealous omnipotence to which his free love is totally subordinated. So it is not surprising that when he finds he can be human without God, modern man rejects God as the enemy of his true freedom. It is quite different if one understands God's omnipotence as the power of his love. 'Love alone is all-powerful. So we must see the rule of God's mercy in his Lordship and consequently the rule of his grace in his justice.'[8]

It is indeed proper to the conviction of faith to state that man cannot exist without God. But in our age of indifference, we need to reinterpret the *anthropological* role of God. The necessity of God is very feeble while it is understood on the level of 'utility'. But if we set the gratuitousness of God against this necessity, we are not inevitably bound to throw God into the realm of arbitrariness. God is non-necessary, since 'God comes from God'. He is the unconditioned being. But as he is out of reach of the opposition between necessity and contingency, it is legitimate to say that God is at once *gratuitous* and *more than necessary*. This invites us to investigate further the ontological specificity of God's being, that is to draw all the consequence from the final Revelation of the Word on the Cross.

(ii) It is not only God's anthropological function that has to be reinterpreted, but his *social* function as well, at least as seen in some traditional theology. Has the all-powerful and providential God of metaphysical theism not served as an ideological backstop for a particular form of society which reflected the unchangeable order of the world as created by God? Theological discourse never exists in a pure state: there is a history of representations of God and therefore of names given to him which is not unrelated to the interests and power structures of a social grouping at any particular moment. In the light of Marxist criticism of ideologies, we are now better able to see when theology becomes degraded into ideology and turns into a system of social justification and legitimation imposing a particular social or political system in the name of the Word of God, when in fact it merely upholds the interests of the dominant group. So, for example, it is the achievement of liberation theologians to have denounced the ambiguity of an official theology which played the game of those in power and so tended to support the *status quo* of an unjust social system.[9]

So we need go beyond the utilitarian version of God and take a fresh look at the gratuitousness of the biblical God as he reveals himself in the *Alliance*, which is exchange, gift and love, excess and generosity. Otherwise, in the eyes of indifferent modern society, the question of God will seem old-fashioned or no longer valid.

There is no doubt that contemporary Christianity has a better understanding of its historic responsibility towards man and society. In many countries in the Third World, the Church is becoming the obvious focus of the hope of the poor and finding that it can no longer dissociate evangelisation in the strict sense from service of man in its Mission. This is not to say that the Christian message should no longer be proclaimed to men as *marked by gratuitousness*. The efficacy of Christianity cannot be said to be exhausted in its efficacy for the world. If it were, it would run the risk of becoming no more than an ideology dedicated to the advancement of mankind and the transformation of the world. This is the limitation of, for example, the non-sacrificial reinterpretation of Christianity put forward by René Girard, that it goes back to being a too utilitarian concept, as though the Christian message of non-violence were the only means by which humanity could escape the collective suicide threatened by nuclear weapons.[10] The Christian Revelation is not only a key to exposing the social mechanics of violence; it is the revelation of the uniqueness of God's free gift.

(b) The originality of a different God

Our context of religious indifference invites us, then, to look for God afresh beyond the categories of usefulness or uselessness; to rediscover, that is, the originality of the God of biblical Revelation.

I have already pointed to the misuse which has been made of the distinction between 'faith' and 'religion' for purposes of argument. But this distinction, in the theological form worked out by Karl Barth, has a most valuable educative function to perform, in that it helps to point out the originality of the God of biblical faith through his *difference* from the gods of pagan religions and the God of theism. The God of the cosmic religions in particular is a God who fits in too neatly with man's needs. He favours man's tendency to evasion by seeking a destiny outside real life. Now given the cultural context of mankind come of age and indifference to religion, the image of a God who 'makes up for man's inadequacies' or 'acts as stopgap for his wants' can only be rejected. As Bonhoeffer said: 'God is not reassuring background music to my life.' He is not a sort of auxiliary engine to help me face up to the contradictions of existence. In this respect, the believer is in the same boat as the unbeliever.

If we take the evidence of biblical revelation about God seriously, we find that the times when men made themselves gods, whether of fertility or of immortality, are just the times when God is not with them. Let us say that God is not in the prolonging of ineffable experiences of which man is capable. He asks to be met in a *history*. And faith, as opposed to religious need, is always the response to an initiative from God, to a movement coming from God towards men.

From the point of view of the comparative history of religions, it has been said that the great pagan religions are religions of *manifestation*, which means that their followers long to find God's traces in the natural elements, in theophanies. In other words, discovering God is no different from experiencing the sacred: God is interpreted in terms of being, or presence, of immanence. What typifies the religion of Israel, on the other hand, is that it is a religion not of manifestation, but of *proclamation*.[11] God does not show himself in the happenings of nature, but in history and in the words of the prophets. The sacredness of nature gives way to stress on the word and ethical commandments.

So, without simplifying excessively, one can conclude that religions, those of yesterday and the new ones of today, always exploit the machine for making gods that is the megalomania of human desire or man's taste for ineffable experiences. But faith, far from being the victory of human desire like religion, is first overcome by a meeting, an otherness, even when that otherness runs counter to human spontaneity. The God of Abraham, Isaac and Jacob, the God of history, the 'utterly other', is the God who creates the question of salvation in man, and the God whose reply completely surpasses human expectation.

What we need to know is whether modern man, for whom the word 'God' has become *meaningless*, is defined only by what is 'available' to him or by a mysterious opening-out to an irreducible *Otherness*, which he is led to by his experiences of the most unforeseeable gratuitousness. Not God as the object of an immediate need or desire, but as the object of a disinterested desire beyond satisfaction. The least inadequate way of expressing this irruption of God into history and into my life, seems to be to re-use Emmanuel Levinas's term, the 'exteriority' of God. Exteriority of God in the sense that

God makes me escape from the unbroken totality of history and the unbroken totality of my immanence wrapped up in itself. God as 'exteriority' is he who makes me break out of the fateful circle of immanence or the inexorable unfolding of a history that is nothing more than endless repetition of the same thing. There is a way out, a break, and this is what we mean by the word 'God'. This is why we should teach the 'Godless' people of our age to call on God as another name for the *freedom* and *grace* in their lives. They should discover God as an 'anti-fate'.

(c) A God who lets himself be driven to the Cross

The pervading religious indifference of our contemporaries is not just a result of the world come of age finding the question of God meaningless. It also feeds on the old objection to God, that he 'allows' evil to flourish in all its forms in a strife-torn world. We are in a historical situation in which the excess of evil, of violence, of injustice never ceases to grow. Faced with such a situation, theism becomes derisory. And the unjustifiable nature of evil sends us back to the most radical element in Christianity—the crucified God.

So, beyond both theism and atheism, we are driven back on the *theologia crucis*. The atheism that shapes our modern age obliges us to work out a new Christian concept of God. Atheism as negation of theism is a turning-point in Christian theology. A theology of the Cross is not only something needed as a response to our situation of religious indifference; it alone is capable of tackling the formidable question of God's justice in the world. It was first Hegel's achievement, and then Bonhoeffer's, to have put forward a *theological* interpretation of atheism, by showing the *christological* origin of modern thinking on 'the death of God'.

To round off these reflections on the nature of God in a context of religious indifference, I should simply like to indicate a course of investigation that seems to me extremely promising: the way in which Bonhoeffer tried to interpret the absence of God in the world from a christological standpoint.

The presupposition for the absence of God is a world *come of age*. This is why it is necessary to abandon the idea of God as a working hypothesis. This is not only a question of intellectual integrity; it is the necessary starting-point for an inner conversion, *coram Deo*. It is a question of recognising 'that we have to live in the world *etsi Deus non daretur*. And this is what we accept as people converted, and therefore before God! God himself forces us to make this avowal. So our coming of age leads us to a truer recognition of our situation before God. God lets us know that we should live like those who lead their lives without God. The God who is with us is the God who abandons us (Mark 15:34). The God who makes us live in the world without God as a working hypothesis is the God before whom we stand for ever. Before God and with God, we live without God.'[12]

This theological interpretation of the fate of absence of God in the world is paradoxical only in appearance. It stems in fact from the specificity of God's being as revealed in the death of God in Jesus on the Cross, the event that enables us to take stock of the presence-absence of God in the world. 'God let himself be driven from the world to the Cross; God in the world is weak and unarmed, and this is how—and only how—he is present to us and helps us. It is quite clear from Matthew 8:17 that Christ does not bring help through his omnipotence, but through his weakness and suffering.'[13]

Bonhoeffer of course turns upside down Feuerbach's classic scheme of things in which man empties himself into an illusory absolute which is God. In the name of biblical revelation, Bonhoeffer daringly puts forward the opposite: God impoverishes himself to enrich man; or even: God dies that man might live. It is religion in general, or rather religiosity, that sends man back to the omnipotence of God (the pagan gods were powers . . .); the Bible, on the other hand, refers men to God's weakness and suffering. In its final Revelation, this is what is shown in the *language of the Cross*.

This bold vision enables us to be beyond the concept of God belonging to the onto-theological tradition which fails to overcome the opposition between God's a-pathetic omnipotence and his extreme vulnerability as shown in the death on the Cross. But it also enables us to form a theological understanding of the original experience of the absence of God in a world indifferent to religion. 'If God allows himself "to be driven from the world", and on the Cross bears the world which would not bear him, then in fact God's being should be thought of as bringing out the alternative between presence and absence.'[14] When we said above that we should live God's absence in the world (*etsi Deus non daretur*) *before God*, this in no way means that we abandon the reality of the presence of God. What we are first and foremost attacking is something that would be only God's *worldly* presence. The theological challenge of religious indifference is to think how God is present even in his absence from the world.

Finally, I would add that a spirituality that takes the fate of God's absence in the world seriously should meditate on the mystery of Jesus being abandoned in his agony. Jesus himself experienced God's silence, and even his *absence*. And it was precisely at that moment that God showed his solidarity with human suffering and death. If our historical situation of religious indifference forces us to think out the *difference* between the God of Jesus and the God of the metaphysical tradition, this must lead us on to show the link between trinitarian theology and the theology of the Cross. In Moltmann's profound words: 'In the forsakenness of the Son the Father also forsakes himself. In the surrender of the Son the Father also surrenders himself, though not in the same way.'[15]

Translated by Paul Burns

Notes

1. See P. Jacquemont, J.-P. Jossua and B. Quelquejeu *Une foi exposée* (Paris 1972).
2. On this point see the French summary E. Schillebeeckx made of his theological methodology in *Expérience humaine et foi en Jésus-Christ* (Paris 1981), esp. pp. 29-64.
3. For a rigorous statement of this *analogy*, see P. Gisel *Vérité et histoire. La théologie dans la modernité* (Paris 1977).
4. M. Belliet *Le Point critique* (Paris 1970) p. 88.
5. The expression is used by J. B. Metz in 'Unbelief as a theological problem' in *Concilium* 6 (June 1965) 32-41.
6. E. Jüngel *Gott als Geheimnis der Welt* (Tubingen 1977) p. 16ff.
7. A. Delzant *La Communication de Dieu* (Paris 1978) p. 22.
8. Jüngel, the work cited in note 6, pp. 26-27.
9. For a broader development of this point, see C. Geffré 'La Crise du Théisme' in *Le Supplément* 122 (1977) 357-379.
10. See in particular the two latest works by R. Girard, *Des Choses cachées depuis la fondation du monde* (Paris 1978) and *Le Bouc émissaire* (Paris 1982).
11. See P. Ricoeur 'Manifestation et proclamation' in *Le Sacré* (Paris 1974) pp. 57-76.
12. D. Bonhoeffer *Widerstand und Ergebung* (Munich 1970).
13. Bonhoeffer, *ibid.* See the commentary by E. Jüngel on these famous passages, in the work cited in note 6, pp. 74-83.
14. Jüngel, the work cited in note 6, p. 81.
15. J. Moltmann *The Crucified God* (London 1974) p. 243 (tr. of *Der gekreuzigte Gott* (Munich 1973)).

PART III

Bulletins

Ignace Berten

The Cardijn Seminary Enterprise: A Road to Faith Among the Working Class

1. A WORKERS' SCHOOL OF FAITH

IN THE French-speaking Regions of Belgium, Wallonia and Brussels, socialism developed among the industrial working classes in reaction against the middle classes, Christian or liberal, and became by far the dominant political creed. Traditionally, it is highly anti-clerical. Most Catholics and the Church itself as an institution remained detached from, suspicious of, and even frankly hostile to the workers' struggle. A small section of the working class has nevertheless remained Christian; in this the JOC (Young Christian Workers) has been an important force since the 1930s. For the most part, the industrial working classes are non-practising, though they usually have a church ceremony for events like weddings and funerals. In country areas by contrast, more traditional religious practice has continued, since villages have preserved their—increasingly threatened—unity and the parish acts as a focal point.

Today, church attendance is in decline, and among the working classes, the Church is coming to seem more and more alien. The liturgical reforms have often been forced on them, sometimes clumsily, and services have become more intellectual and abstract. For the few remaining members of the working classes who had kept links with the Church, this has been a further alienating factor, reinforcing the split that occurred in the nineteenth century.

It was against this background that the Cardinal Cardijn Seminary was founded. Its aim was to allow a number of working men to become priests without the secondary education the diocesan seminaries required. It was originally set up on the same lines as standard seminaries, with resident students and full-time teaching (and 'adapted', i.e., popularised, theology); however, in the fifteen years since then, it has changed considerably. The first move was to keep candidates in half-time employment; then to keep them in uninterrupted full-time employment throughout their training and after ordination. In consequence, residence at the seminary was abolished, evening and week-end training was introduced, and there was geographical decentralisation, with the training staff going out to the students; in the original quarters at Jumet, a working-class suburb of Charleroi, only a secretariat now remains. All this led to training methods being thoroughly and continually reviewed, an inductive process

F   71

based on structured analysis of experience, its human implications and its connection with the Gospel. These changes gave rise to a further fundamental change, when working-class lay men and women asked to join in, a step which contributed greatly to strengthening the movement that was beginning to take shape. Regional training groups were then formed, consisting mainly of lay people among whom a few candidates for the priesthood were trained. About twenty such groups are now active. There are also some continuing groups centred on particular commitments, for people who want further training. Nearly 400 adults, including industrial and agricultural workers, non-manual workers, non-working mothers, etc., are involved, with men and women in about equal numbers. About twenty, celibate men, are preparing for the priesthood.

Space does not permit me to describe the methods of work or the training materials that have been elaborated and are being constantly revised,[1] the distribution of duties or the forms of participation, etc. But there are some aspects of the groups which are important for the theme of this article and so must be emphasised.

The Seminary was founded in 1967, that is to say, shortly after the Council, at a time marked by the optimism of *Gaudium et Spes*, the ferment of May 1968, the Allende experiment in Chile and the beginnings of liberation theology. At that time, training was strongly influenced by the militant trade union and political outlook and had an active vision of social change: underlying it was a buoyant conviction that in the short or medium term, ongoing history could be controlled from a working-class base and guided into self-directing socialism. The tools of social analysis were studied, particularly from the economic point of view; there was reflection and evaluation of action. The guide-line was the domination–liberation axis. Guides to Scripture along these lines were elaborated. There was a common effort to re-express or just to discover the meaning of Jesus Christ and to celebrate faith in accordance with this work and political view.

The Church, too, in the concrete form of the parishes through which it was usually encountered, was subjected to the same process of analysis and questioning. This led to two different reactions. People who belonged to parishes, among them some catechists or active members of various Christian movements, and who had felt relatively at home there, became more critical and began to speak out more, in solidarity with their milieu; at times this led to difficulties, and some people cut their connection. The second reaction was that of people who had completely given up regular practice: they turned to the Seminary, motivated by questions about faith or by attachment to Jesus or the Gospel; this group discovered that a particular way of being the Church was meaningful. Both sets discovered that it was possible to be the Church differently and to celebrate differently. They called then for new and freer places where they could speak and celebrate their faith undivorced from their real-life experience and their militancy. This was the first stage in the development of grass-roots Christian communities.

Given the approach which had been adopted, 'heavy' militants, i.e., men and women who were very militantly involved in trade unions or politics, naturally came to dominate the groups, one of the few places where they could express the link between their faith and militancy—which they did forcefully. This meant that the many less politicised or less staunch forms of commitment were to some extent devalued.

However, the preponderance of the 'heavy' militants and the sometimes over-narrow emphasis on a socio-political and economic approach were to be weakened by a series of questions and by events in the socio-economic sphere.

Questions connected with the relation between affectivity, sexuality and militancy; about the relation between men and women at work, in the home, in the Church and even in the Seminary itself; problems about the schooling and upbringing of children; frequent contacts with the Third World, and Latin America in particular; experience of 'alternative' production and consumption and contact with the ecological movement were all very influential in bringing about a change of approach.

The economic climate had a similar effect. The beginning of the 1970s was doubly a time of hope: it was thought that the dynamic of growth would continue indefinitely, and that it was possible for the workers to unite in order to obtain or impose a more just distribution of the benefits of growth. But today we have economic and political crises and their effects: unemployment rising mercilessly; increasing concessions having to be made; hard-won guarantees being threatened, and purchasing power diminishing. Against this background, it is harder to know what line of action to take, and to maintain solidarity.

2. TOWARDS GRASS-ROOTS COMMUNITIES

Solitude, isolation and all the many problems of life today are creating an ever-increasing demand for focal meeting points with a stronger community basis. Existing institutions and movements, however essential, cannot meet this need suitably even when they work well in the light of their own aims. Expectations are immense: mutual support and help, common rejoicing, sharing questions and difficulties, guiding and training young people, and, as Christians, sharing and celebrating faith, linking life and action with Jesus Christ, reading Scripture together, etc. Initial steps are taken, groups are formed and develop in various places. These young growths are pointers to one possible way forward.

These groups bring together militants who have retained what is often an uneasy connection with the institutional Church of the parishes, and others who have severed the link through disappointment, discouragement, disgust or even revolt at a Church in which they can see neither welcome nor solidarity. They bring together people who still frequent the parish church but find additional enrichment in the group, and others whom organised religion leaves cold, who never go near a church, but for whom God or Jesus Christ mean something; for them a group has meaning, and celebrating with it contributes to the meaning. Others, too, are brought together by the groups: people in irregular situations who, spurned and guilt-ridden, have been shut out or feel shut out by the disdain and opprobrium of church people and have never resigned themselves to being deprived of sacramental life. For them, the group opens up a space where at long last they can breathe.

3. A WORKING PARTY: 'THE FAITHS THAT GIVE US LIFE'

Today's difficult state of affairs has focused attention on questions about meaning, centred on faith as a vitalising force. How, when despondency and fatalism are growing daily worse, and more and more militants are cracking up or giving in, can one keep going, stay alive, go on believing and hoping, and come back fighting after every failure?

A theological research group working on the theme 'the faiths that give us life' has been set up to try to answer these questions. At its last annual assessment and planning weekend in June 1982, a member of the group reported progress so far. The following extracts from the report give a good picture of the working party's aim and method:

'If one is not to be defeated by the struggles and difficulties of life and the threats our society is faced with, but keep going in spite of failures and not lose hope though things and people are so slow to react . . . one has to be sustained by some faith, to have a sound inner strength.

Some say: it is my Christian faith, or my faith in God, or my faith in Jesus Christ that keeps me going. Others, with whom they work and fight side by side, will say: it is my faith in man.

Are belief in Jesus, in God, in man or in life all the same thing? If not, what is the difference between them? What is the reality behind the different words and forms of expression?

The theological working party set itself to go more deeply into these questions. (. . .)

It decided to avoid abstract discussion and concentrate on personal witness and the way the questions are experienced. Each person in turn makes a statement, which the others listen to without interrupting. If need be, questions will be asked in order to clarify a point, but there is no discussion. In the report, one of the group leaders gives an analytical account of the meeting and reformulates some of what was said in order to bring out both the similarities and the differences behind the varied individual wording. This acts as the starting-point for another stage. (. . .)

The process needs an atmosphere of complete trust. There is a general understanding—which can be sensed almost tangibly—that nothing is taboo and no dogma is beyond criticism. Everyone speaks freely about his certainties and difficulties. We listen to the other, let him take his time, go part of the way with him . . . and that allows him to "read" his life. The work is not static, however. There is constant interaction: the real intense group-listening makes every member of the group question his own deepest being, dig still deeper, and share. Moreover, the work of the group is much more than the sum of the individuals it is made up of.

Time plays an important part in the group process. We have to be able to let each individual go at his own pace; so we allow the time for this. This year the group has had five meetings, each of which lasted from 3 p.m. to 8 p.m. And as we are nowhere near having exhausted the basic questions, we shall continue next year.

Till now the work has been centred on two main points:

(a) What is my mainspring? What keeps me going today and makes me always bounce back and start again? Something in myself? Something in others? God? Jesus Christ? And what is it that makes the spring break? (b) How are God and Jesus Christ a mainspring for me in my concrete situation today? What can I say about God or Jesus Christ on the basis of my own experience?

It is impossible at present to summarise the statements. The main lines of inquiry are clear, but they have accumulated a wide range of material. More progress will be needed before any synthesis is attempted.

It is, however, possible to make one observation, which is that the dividing-line is not between believers and non-believers, Christians and non-Christians, religious and non-religious, but within each of these groups. Within any given set of people that we try to contrast with another set, we find on the one side fatalism—under whatever name—and on the other side, those who believe man has just that little extra and that there is more to every man than can be seen. Perhaps the dividing-line passes through us too?

The next stage has been prepared in outline. (. . .) Further questions are envisaged, e.g., how to express one's life-giving faith in communities where faiths may be very varied; whether belief in Jesus Christ is desirable for all; the meaning of life, suffering and death; whether the Gospel and politics are connected.'

4. WAYS FORWARD, BELIEFS AND PROBLEMS

(a) An education in faith: the opening up of a road

The Seminary's training groups are fairly mixed. The members are all from the lower classes, have not much education, have some kind of commitment and are motivated by a question about faith. But on the last point they differ widely: there are church goers and non-church goers; traditional religious ideas and very secularised, even agnostic, attitudes; tranquil faith and guilt-ridden scrupulosity; positive Church membership and indifference, aggression or rancour towards the Church. . . .

The basic principle is to start with day-to-day experience and attempt to reflect on and analyse it, using a method—the fruit of fifteen years' experience—that the group leaders suggest. Religious experience and statement have a place in the scheme if they emerge of themselves, but they are not directly solicited at the beginning. Systematic reflection about Jesus Christ only comes much later, though matters of faith may already have been touched on several times depending on the particular group's dynamic.

One of the first educational aims is to get each member to speak freely about his experience, what he believes or does not believe and the questions that worry him or on which he has got stuck. There is a basic contract: there will be no criticism. What others say will be listened to because it is what is real for them. This does not prevent clashes.

This open, non-authoritarian dynamic gradually allows the group to express its faith. Here again the principle that there will be no criticism applies. The leader never lays down what must be believed. If he is asked what the Church teaches about something, he does not elude the question, but always gives his personal opinion as a believer too, saying what he himself now believes and how he would put it in his own words, or how it has been seen in the past. If everyone is allowed gropingly to say what he really believes or does not believe and what his questions and doubts are, each member of the group and the group as a whole can get further, and come both to question things that were sometimes naïvely accepted as obvious, and to discover that there is some point in things they had not bothered with or had even definitively dismissed. . . . We always find after a few years that nearly everyone comes to enjoy and be interested in group reading of the Bible, that Jesus Christ becomes an important point of reference, and that celebrating together becomes meaningful.

The working classes have only a limited vocabulary, and speak concretely; fact and deeds mean more to them than speeches, which they distrust. To reach the point of being able to express themselves in their own type of language, and to analyse, is a liberation. It requires a process of abstraction, but one that is only meaningful if it remains in constant touch with everyday experience. Many trade unions, political groupings and other groups have ended up talking so abstractly and analytically that the militants cannot be understood by their own people. The aim of the Seminary is to enable members of the groups to express the faith in their own words and speak about it among their own people without having to use two different languages. If faith needs 'translating' before it can be shared with and understood by someone from the same background, then either the speaker has left his own culture behind him, or else the faith is not yet a living part of that culture and background.

If they are judged on their abstract content, against dogmatic formulae or the catechism, the statements that may be made in this way will seem inadequate or perhaps even heretical to some. . . . But if, on the contrary, one has the eyes to see that indifference, suspicion, ready-made formulae and routine gestures have been replaced by personal expression of faith, by practice and by sacraments which come after lengthy group preparation, etc.; and if one can penetrate behind the words and see what the actions, the attitudes and the life-stories are saying, one will see faith made manifest and giving life, and there will be rejoicing.

(b) The question of meaning

We have already shown how the theological study group 'the faiths that give us life' is important for the whole Seminary, but its wider import must also be discussed.

The state of society today, with the collapse of what could be called the 'material' sense of life that has dominated the whole of Western society in recent years, is raising a basic question of meaning. This 'material' sense rests on a number of characteristic ideas: the idea of continuous progress, with the expectation that tomorrow will bring better living conditions and more goods, means of transport and communication than today; the idea of social mobility upwards, with the hope of rising a few rungs in the social ladder; the idea that the whole social community gradually benefits from the rise in the gross national product and economic and technical development, so that though social inequalities exist, people nevertheless feel that they are getting closer to the class above them because they can now acquire what used to be the preserve of higher classes.

This material sense is now collapsing. Many people see progress as having ceased and even gone into reverse; they foresee that technical progress will continue but that it will not be of equal benefit to all, and that the threat of deprivation and rejection hangs over everyone. Ever-increasing numbers of people—far from evenly drawn from different sections of society—are being affected by unemployment and suddenly falling several rungs down the social ladder. The outlook is bleak, not hopeful, and young people as a whole feel that this society holds no future for them.

The failure of the myth of continuous growth seems to have left economists with no means of effectively controlling the situation. Purely economic solutions aimed at putting public finance on a sounder footing and diminishing the balance of payments deficit are very costly in social and political terms and of very dubious efficacy.

The problem of meaning thus arises in all its nakedness. What position is one to take when the situation is out of control and political plans seem unlikely to be very effective in the short or medium term? How and in the name of what is one to go on fighting and attempting to keep the idea of a better world alive when the whole future is a gamble and the most immediate challenge is just to stay alive?

This question has direct relevance for the Church. When science, modernism and democracy offered the world a hope of liberation, the Church resisted them strongly. But in the end it went over to them (though in part only, because it has still not really accepted the demand for autonomous human responsibility), and adopted almost unquestioningly the ideal of progress and growth. The optimism of Vatican II, and of *Gaudium et Spes* in particular, is based on this outlook. Material development is part of humanity's progress towards a more fully human life; it is therefore part of God's plan for the kingdom. But when this vision of material growth begins to be equated with the progress of the human race, a problem arises, particularly if the human and social cost of growth for other sections of the population and other regions and countries is ignored, because the bourgeois conception of growth is individualistic in approach. Just how far the Church has been contaminated by this idea of growth can be seen in the way it so often refuses to recognise social conflict and confrontation and to accept any analysis based on the class struggle—which it nevertheless recognised in the nineteenth century as a reality imposed by the rich and powerful!

The situation today invites us to re-read the gospels creatively. Jesus lived in a society that rejected people in the name of the false god of legal and ritual purity. He established a new realm of meaning and life by a series of acts of solidarity that were also social and religious acts of severance. Our society systematically makes rejects of people in the name of the false gods of profitability and economic laws, and subjects whole sections of society to humiliation and scorn. In the name of what is one to hazard the acts of solidarity and severance that could open up a new realm of meaning and life and so accomplish the offer made by the God of Jesus Christ? This is without doubt one of the most vital questions which must be answered by the collective research now being done by the Seminary.

(c) Non-religious language and popular religion

The people who come to the Seminary have Christian roots, but some of them have rejected traditional Christian words. Terms like 'Church', 'priest', 'sacrament' represent for them the very negation of liberation and human dignity. This attitude is very widespread in working-class society because of the use to which the Church has put these words. With these people there is in the groups the constant problem of how to live and speak the message of the Gospel when the accepted terms are incendiary. It takes time, patience and self-restraint to cope with this problem, and is not always easy, since some people can speak about God or Jesus Christ much more readily than others. To be obliged to keep quiet when one is training faith-leaders is frustrating; it must be done, however, if the group is one day to express its faith together. But it is also a fruitful experience, which makes one see more clearly than one's own occasional personal experience with others, the world or life can do, how ambiguous the public images and the religious language one was brought up to are. There are clerics confident in their own learning who would be disconcerted and even scandalised if they witnessed this self-restraint and silence. . . .

The Seminary meets another aspect of working-class life which on the surface contradicts the non-religious approach, i.e., the many expressions of popular religion, found among the less young in particular. People will often no longer be practising, but still have Church christenings, first communions, marriages and funerals, and will occasionally go on a pilgrimage or light a candle to some saint. On these occasions there is often no connection between the priest's words and the people's actions, yet for the people, the actions are not just a social custom; they matter because they reflect a connection between life and 'something else', God. Since many of these practices have recently been discredited, a lot of people have abandoned the Church completely, while others continue with the practices, but more or less secretly or ashamedly. The people who ask for education about the faith have usually distanced themselves somewhat from popular religion; they feel more at home in small group services where the externals of liturgy have changed considerably and personal expression plays a major part. How can their experiences and actions be linked to what most of the others expect, which also in its way emerges as a vehicle of truth and meaning?

Moreover, though the call for grass-roots communities is very urgent, it raises a difficult problem. The needs it meets are not specific to Christians. But there is often a Christian initiative behind a move towards more community-based solidarity. And for Christians, the liturgy is often the centre and kingpin of the community. What then should be the group's relation with the wider, in effect pluralist, community; what should its focal point be; and how should the search for and the sharing of meaning of be actively pursued? The problem has been opened up and is often met with, but as yet little progress has been made.

(d) Ministries and training for ministries

The Cardijn Seminary was founded to make it possible for some workers to become priests, and this is still one of its main tasks. But it is part of a broader prospect of the future: the hope that one day a Church of the workers will come into being. This would not be a separate Church, or opposed to the institutional Church. But it is undeniable that the Church of Jesus Christ has never really been part of working-class society in this part of Europe. Its institutions, its public image and its personnel have been overwhelmingly bourgeois and middle class. What the Seminary wants is to allow a sister Church to emerge, in communion with and complementing the other, but with all the confrontations in truth it would involve too. (In Jerusalem, we read in *Acts*, Jews and Greeks set up two different and partly autonomous organisations; the autonomy was the condition that made it possible for the Gospel to become a living part of Greek culture.)

The scheme for workers' ecclesial communities that can celebrate their faith and life in the Eucharist has been officially recognised as necessary by various dioceses, but is running into countless difficulties and finding itself blocked. One reason for this is that the diocesan authorities lack the political will to accept the real consequences of such a scheme because they are obsessed with unity, are afraid to let go of any power, and fear conflict. Another reason is that rulings by Rome systematically block the question of ministries.

The Eucharist is what makes a community Christian; this is affirmed in theory by the Church and found to be so by communities. But increasing numbers of communities are being deprived of the Eucharist for lack of a minister. In practice, this raises once again the question of the presidency of the Eucharist.

From this point of view the situation today is utterly paradoxical. People are coming together and the seeds of grass-roots communities are beginning to germinate. This is not a spontaneous occurrence, but the result of long and patient work by faith-leaders. Many of the latter are priests, but others are lay people; in which case there is often no priest available—or able to talk to people in the language of their daily lives and thus of their faith—so the group cannot celebrate its faith by the Eucharist. How long must this vital need go on being sacrificed to the canonical rules of a Church which frequently knows nothing about grass-roots Christian experience?

There is also a significant development to be noted among some of the workers who were ordained priest after being trained by the Seminary. They remained in employment and worked for years at bringing people together, giving them a lead, and at times celebrating with groups. Then gradually, communities began to take shape. The priests now needed more time because there were more requests for guidance and more initiatives to be taken or kept up. So some of the priests then began to ask themselves whether they ought to leave their employment in order to cope with these demands. Thus, by request, we are back with the notion of a full-time ministry, prepared for not by the traditional training but by years of work at the grass-roots. Meanwhile there are lay people, men or women, with the same skills and experience and the same faith, ready and able to take on the work.

CONCLUSION

It is clear from the experience of the Cardijn Seminary that, against the general background of religious indifference and distrust of the Church, it is possible to open up a road to faith among the working classes. It is not the only possible road, nor is the Seminary alone in suggesting a move of this kind in Wallonia and Brussels. Given certain conditions, it can succeed.

The Seminary's aim is to train group leaders; it is only indirectly concerned with the mass of the working class since its public is made up of people who are strongly motivated to begin with. Its belief is that in the long term the working class will be evangelised from within, by leaders it will itself produce. There are signs today, in the various steps towards the formation of grass-roots communities by people trained at the Seminary, that its belief can be realised. This result is the fruit of years of patient presence. The steps can be taken because we trust people and let the groups themselves find their own forms of expression and celebration.

The leaders who want it are offered the support of meetings where experience can be evaluated and exchanged, and it is accepted that mistakes and blunders can occur; where they will not be judged or condemned but helped to assess what they are doing. These meetings can be seen to lead to a deepening of understanding.

The communities usually have a very strong wish to be part of the Church and to be recognised as such. They are stamped with the constant struggle of the working class to affirm its own dignity and obtain greater justice; they therefore see themselves as being in conflict with most other Christian communities in so far as the latter are composed mainly of people from the class they are fighting against in their everyday lives. But that in no way lessens their desire to belong and to be recognised: the other communities are not the whole Church. It is for this reason that what bishops do and say is of particular significance for encouraging, disappointing or angering them. . . . In general, unfortunately, because it is their difference that is noticed most, they meet disquiet and distrust rather than a warm and patient welcome or rejoicing at their infant promise.

There is a chance for the Church in the working class today: the Gospel is capable of being good news. But will the institutional Church dare take a leap in the dark and risk letting the Gospel loose for people to hear and read it by themselves?

Translated by Ruth Murphy

Note

1. The following documentation about working methods and materials is available and may be obtained from the Secrétariat of the Séminaire Cardinal Cardijn, 136 rue Puissant, 6040 Jumet, Belgium: *Luttes et Foi* (Brussels 1980) (an account of a series of weekend meetings organised by the Seminary); *Dossier no. 1* (a short account of the enterprise); *Dossier no. 5: Jésus et la libération humaine*, 256 pages; *L'Evangile de Marc, quelques clefs de lecture* (suggests a method for reading St Mark).

Jean Collet

Images of Indifference, Indifference to Images. Audio-Visual Media and Contemporary Indifference

AN IMAGE. In a few years it has become familiar. Silhouettes of boys and girls, sometimes of adults, passed in the street or the subway, with light earphones on their heads and a little box at their waists. They move about in a cloud of music, alien, *indifferent*.

Hypothesis. Is there perhaps not a link between the amazing development of modern technologies—in particular the means of transmitting image and sound, audio-visual media—and indifference? What indifference? After all, is the cultivated man, the 'sage', who sits down in a library and buries himself in a book, so far from our young person with the 'Walkman'? Reading, listening to a concert, looking at a view, watching a film, means first isolating oneself, cutting oneself off from the surrounding noise, withdrawing. Is the indifference of the person with the Walkman really different in kind from that of the philosopher concentrating in his study, of the pop fan in the discotheque?

At this point we ought to scrutinise the word 'indifferent', which can be a trap. On the one hand it denotes the person who is insensitive, who shows no interest. On the other it refers to what is equal, neutral, similar, what presents no difference. Another word is needed for this. 'Undifferentiated', for example. We see at once that while the 'Walkman' buffs may be indifferent to what is happening around them, on the other hand they are not like the others. They are alone in the middle of the crowd. We notice them. Singular and so different. One day perhaps, when we all go around each with our little earphones, we shall achieve, in all senses of the term, 'indifference'. We shall be doubly, totally indifferent. This achieved indifference is something we already experience when we are in our cars, listening to the radio in the middle of a traffic jam, or when we watch television at home. In his film *Play-time* Jacques Tati showed the residents of an apartment block all engaged in watching the same television programme at the same time. The camera climbed up the glass façade revealing, with a desolating monotony, the similarity of situations, gestures, reactions. We laughed at it, of course, because we recognised ourselves and were afraid.

The person with the Walkman makes us afraid too. Protected by their helmet, girded around with wires, they resemble those science fiction characters, cosmonauts, voyagers in space, lunar heroes confronting an environment which is airless, inhuman, polluted, threatening. They are protecting themselves. Just as we are protecting ourselves when we switch on the car radio to help us tolerate a road on which the cars are nose-to-tail without moving. In that situation we escape on the spot, through imagination. Dreaming replaces movement. Here I see in my mind Marcello Mastroianni with his car stuck in an underpass at the beginning of Fellini's film *8½*. Anxious looks at the occupants of the other cars, remote, silent as ghosts. Suffocation. 'I must get out of here at all costs.' The hero of the film dreams that he is flying away very high, hovering like a great bird above a deserted beach. The parable of the solitary crowd, each individual shut up in his or her shell, protected by their own little music, isolated in the silence of their daydreams or their nightmares. All alike, undifferentiated and indifferent.

These images can easily be painted blacker, but I cannot bring myself to take them tragically, let alone interpret them as signs of a modern disease. At all times the person who separated himself from the crowd passed for a mad person or a sage, for a monster or a saint. The fact that we are more than ever condemned to this separation, to this withdrawal, this flight, shouldn't worry us that much. It could even be held that a retreat is the necessary preliminary to better communication. We must first isolate ourselves, cross the desert, in order to make contact with others by new paths. Perhaps art is simply the constant attempt to take this detour anew, the refusal of a contact which has become routine, immediate, impoverished. A break. The invention of a language, a tool, a medium, an approach, never before used. We need to lose ourselves to find ourselves. Art = apart. Abandoning the norm and the rule, hazarding a false step which may become the very movement to bring us to the other. Art = articulation, understood as a better, more supple, truer articulation.

We have come a long way from indifference, from our double indifference, that of the dreamer who is present without being present, who thinks he or she is escaping, setting themselves apart, and who is being merged with everyone. The dreamer in *8½* is an artist. He is not just displaying his treasured indifference amid our traffic jams. He is moving. He is tracing a route, a hesitant, anxious route, between the crowd which harasses him and his inaccessible dream. He plots a course between heaven and earth and invites us to follow him in that perilous exploration. He is thus completely different in the sense that he is always elsewhere, multiplying separations to turn them into articulations, provoking breaks which will become links.

This would make indifference simply a false start in communication. A false move which remains a false move—and so leads to nothing? Let us try a different approach.

What is the person with the Walkman listening to? Mozart, Gregorian chant or disco music? Poems or variety? Sooner or later we come back to the old story of Aesop's tongue: there are no good or bad tools of communication. The media are 'the best of things, the worst of things'. The only important question is: What is being said? It is a matter of content, programmes. There is a quality of listening or looking which depends on the quality of the discourse, the image, the spectacle. Alas, we all know that the most sincere or most profound words may provoke deadly boredom, just as the most elaborate TV programmes are ignored by the majority of viewers; in the cinema how many masterpieces have met the indifference of the pubic? No-one has ever found the recipe for 'good communication'. Only one thing is certain: it is not a matter of technique or content. We must start again, look somewhere else for the indifference which is bothering us.

News on television. Images of war. Not that long ago the Vietnam war. Closer to us the Beirut massacres. Unbearable images which provoke horror, shame and indignation. Powerful images which damn politicians. No one today denies the influence of American television on the development of the Vietnam war. At last indifference cracks. Confronted with blatant injustice on the small screen, we react.

But what if this example, instead of reassuring us, about ourselves and the beneficial effects of television, proved its narcotic power? We are dealing with an extreme case, catastrophe, the spectacle of violent death. Here television wakes us up. Let us change the metaphor to another technology of communication, the motorway. The motorway is no more than a strip of road to be got along uneventfully, a machine for eliminating space, countryside, time. But it only takes an accident, disaster, and we wake, we stop, we remember.

Road, TV, walkman, machines for producing indifference. It takes nothing less than death to break indifference. There will be objections. Television programmes are made up of a variety of genres, documentaries, news, reports, discussions, comedy, films. All observers and sociologists agree that viewers choose their programme. In other words they differentiate. But immediately we find that in the most dissimilar countries viewers select the same proportions of these different types of programme. The constancy is astonishing: fiction always accounts for about 50 per cent of the time devoted to TV (with variations of plus or minus 2 per cent). In other words, television is a cocktail whose composition does not vary from one country to another, from one regime to another, from one culture to another.[1]

Can we still talk about culture when we are in the presence of such uniformity? What defines a culture is precisely the capacity of human beings to set up differences, that is, meaning, taste, flavour. A culture begins with the choice of food. I like this. I do not like that. This is good, but I don't eat that bread. This is the origin of symbols and symbolism. I recognise myself—I differentiate myself—by belonging to the group which eats in such a way. To speak the same language is first to eat, to savour, with the same tongue. The foods of the spirit are tasted and shared like the foods of the flesh. Lover says to lover, friend to friend, 'I like this book. What about you?'

What about when we all consume the same foods? Ought we to think, like the supporters of Esperanto and some television enthusiasts, that we are moving towards a new Pentecost? The human race united by 'worldvision' in communion through the same programme?

It was possible to believe this, and even to make sermons and speeches on the idea, around the fifties. Today we know that the dream was vain, dangerous. We know that advanced technologies produce indifference all along the line: uniformity in programmes, torpor in attitudes, monotony in habits, loss of symbol and a retreat into the imaginary. We also know that in order to communicate human beings need to mark distances, to establish differences. When there are no more differences, when everything is 'equal', we are forced to reinvent culture by starting from death, the absolute radical difference which is the basis of all the others. That is why television, naturally, has recourse to disaster. Televisual culture begins with road accidents, kidnappings, assassinations and massacres. Violent death is the ultimate sharing. The death given and received, the symbolic act *par excellence*. Primitive, barbaric, sacrificial television. In the age of the small screen and the computer, there are only two types of difference. One is death. Death constitutes the greatest actual difference; it is mysterious and inaccessible. The other is binary logic, the difference between 0 and 1, the unit of information, the smallest difference, abstract, devious and manipulable. On television disaster, the difference between death and life, is the unit of information, the greatest and the only information. Apart from that television is only noise, undifferentiated murmur, a flux of images and sounds without meaning.

Against this background of tumult, in the daunting regression promised us by technology, through the colourless chaos of an information production which has become cancerous, dizzying, how are we to define religious indifference? Not as the death of God or even his absence, but his lack of *meaning*. The fact that the name of God no longer evokes anything at all. Can we understand this in terms of our previous discussion?

First hypothesis. Religious indifference is no more than a foreseeable, logical consequence of generalised indifference. Since everything combines to abolish differences, there is no more room for the divine, the transcendent. With the best intentions in the world, people have been struggling for two or three decades to save God by stressing his humanity. God with us because like us. God in the midst of us, brother-sister, friend, equal. In a society of indifference religion has gone down the inescapable slope of indifference. In the same act it destroyed itself. When everything is equal, alike, there are no more distances. There is nothing to link, no here and no elsewhere. There is no more earth and no more heaven. No more religious dimension.

Second hyphothesis. One is always haunted by what one suppresses. When we neutralise, trivialise, when heaven is confused with earth, when there is no more meaning, we are afraid. We are in the middle of a fog, a situation conducive to phantoms and hallucinations. Shakespeare's plays and Antonioni's films come to mind here. Both of these artists show what happens when mist veils eyes and shapes. There is an undifferentiated space, a tragic space, which calls forth extreme violence, a gesture to separate life and death, being and non-being, at the risk of madness. Antonioni's characters makes us feel with poignant anguish the threat of disappearance, dissolution. The photographer in *Blow-up* thinks he notices a corpse in a shot of a park he has enlarged. Through the grain of the image, the undifferentiated tumult of the photographic emulsion, radical information stands out, absolute difference, the presence of a dead person, of death itself. It is a sublime parable which we find in different forms in every film of Antonioni's. *Identification d'une femme* shows us a film director looking for an actress. He meets two women and tries to see the female character he has created in one of these actresses, but he cannot 'identify' (differentiate) any of these women. A hallucinating scene shows us the hero who has lost his girl-friend in the fog.

Antonioni is perhaps the director who has most strongly felt the effects of a civilisation dominated by images. A film-maker knows that the existence of his characters is determined by light. It is light which gives outline to space and shapes. This light has only to become diffuse, cloudy, and all is over. Creating a character in the cinema is not just a matter of putting him or her on a set, embodying them in the work of an actor or actress. It is first of all bringing them to light, in a direct sense enabling them to be born to the light of day. Here the old metaphors of birth regain their poetic force, washed by ordinary experience. And if we remember that the etymology of *Deus* is also that of 'day' (*dies*), 'light', we see that the technique of the cinema could inspire a theology of our image-based civilisation: God is the mystery which brings us to light. It is what separates our day and night and, by so doing, brings us to birth out of chaos. The genesis of a film and its characters helps us to relive the other Genesis. We *are* only in light and through light.

To create a film is to 'inform' the sensitive emulsion, separate shade and light, relive the old conflict, the eternal battle between day and night.

There is therefore an image pain, which psychoanalysis has investigated and confirmed (the mirror stage). Denis Vasse has written: 'In being born to an image, the human being is born to pain. . . . When I consent to experience pain, I am simply saying, "This experience of the image is mine; it is really me. I am this desire to be everything which deludes itself in its belief. I am also this consciousness of being nothing which tries to recover its position by repossessing everything in an objective knowledge, but at the cost of repressing my primordial desire. Finally, I am that to-and-fro from the one to the other which I now see reflected in the very movement of that image which dissolves before my desire and breaks up in my knowledge." '

Is not indifference to images, the indifference of images (that of the beholder, that of the producers), a way of refusing, denying the pain intrinsic to the image? Is it not a refusal to be born before the image? In other words, it is a refusal to acknowledge our fragility, our dependence. Alternatively, we let ourselves sink deliciously into the image, which has now become purely imaginary, a solvent. This is what I call the sin of Narcissus. And it is clear that most audio-visual productions destroy us like Narcissus. They enfold us in a delightful torpor (Narcissus means 'narcos', narcotic, drug).

The modern cinema and a large part of television have no ambition other than to produce and multiply 'phantasms' into which we escape. Escape, dispersion, the words are eloquent: 'we explode'.

Alternatively we take refuge in an objectivity of images. The image then becomes a pure reflection of reality. It is held at a distance great enough for it no longer to concern us. It is a foreign image, reducible to an item of knowledge. It becomes information, a document, evidence; it is no more than an infinitely manipulable object. I no longer recognise myself in it and so I am no longer afraid of it.

There is thus a double indifference. The indifference which makes me melt into the image, amalgamates me with it and drowns me in it. There is the indifference which keeps me at a distance, forbids me to see myself as different in that mirror, amputates all those parts of me that I do not want to own.

In television programme schedules, with their basic division into fiction and documentaries, shows this double strategy very well. Narcissus is destroyed all the more effectively for being paralysed by the other, by what he believes to be external, foreign to him. Narcissus dies of this painless amputation.

To quote Denis Vasse again: 'For the movement of the image not to remain this pure reflection of me as disjointed which drives me to despair, for it to return me to myself as a subject, double yet still one, I have to be able to recognise in it the movement of another 'I'. The image has to appear to me as an image of the other, an other who is then in me and outside of me, because every image is always mine, in my body; outside of me because the movement of this image is a movement which escapes my grasp.'

The indifference provoked by the constant onrush of images and the bombardment we suffer from the audio-visual media has too often been explained by 'the crisis of identity'. This was another way of flattening the image and making the problem insoluble. I no longer know who I am. How will I ever know if I do not set up, in myself and before myself, the other, if I do not perceive the image as the privileged locus of encounter between the other and me, between myself and myself, between God and me, God who is at once totally Other and already present at the most intimate level of my being?

What the audio-visual media show us is that there is a crisis of otherness. There is a loss of relief, of the third dimension (symbol), the dimension which enables us to come and go in the image, not to be flattened by the image, nor to be alone and remote from it, above it. Indifference = flatness. Jean Baudrillard says, 'When God starts to resemble man, man no longer resembles anything. When Man starts to resemble man, others no longer resemble anything.'

Breaking indifference would mean recovering the Word, not the filling commentary, platitude on platitude, but the symbol which opens, the spirit which gives air and moves. 'Ah, how heavy this world is!' was Céline's reaction the only time he went on television.

Breaking indifference would mean also demystifying production to the benefit of seduction and creation. Production is always re-production, the accumulation of similar objects or shapes, in an obsession with numbers and quantity. To seduce is to create an emptiness, arouse the pain of want and absence, and so the desire which is always the desire for the Other, a call to be reborn, to give life.

Perhaps we must go through indifference, the flat desert of production, to recover a thirst and taste for the Word.

Translated by Francis McDonagh

Note

1. A study published by UNESCO in 1982 under the title *Trois semaines de télévision. Une comparaison internationale.*

Rosino Gibellini

Beyond Atheism: A Dossier of the Secretariat for Non-Believers on Religious Indifference

ON 9TH APRIL 1965 the Secretariat for Non-believers was set up. Its task was well expressed in the title of its quarterly journal *Atheism and Dialogue*, that is, to study the phenomenon of atheism and on the basis of a deeper study which clarifies some of the issues, instigate a dialogue between believers and non-believers. To celebrate a decade of intense activity, the Secretariat has published a large-scale interdisciplinary and interreligious study on an apparently new phenomenon, for which there is no tradition of reflection and study,[1] and which seems to go beyond atheism: religious indifference.[2]

1. ATHEISM AND RELIGIOUS INDIFFERENCE

If *atheism* is the explicit negation of God, if *agnosticism* suspends judgment, has not reached a verdict and therefore has not finally closed the case on the question of God, if *practical atheism* means living as if God did not exist, *religious indifference*—at least in its radical form which we are dealing with here—means lacks of interest in or feeling about God and the religious dimension of existence. The lack of interest is in the sphere of the intelligence, the lack of feeling, that of will. Lack of interest and feeling go with an absence of religious restlessness and a previously expressed judgment about the irrelevance of the question of God. It is a sort of 'religious emptiness', as Vincenzo Miano puts it in the introductory article to the *Dossier*. It implies the final closing of the case and filing away of the question of God. In this sense religious indifference stands at a greater distance from faith than the positions mentioned above, as Andre Charron remarked in his typology of those who are 'distant' from faith: 'As opposed to other non-believers, who do not wish to close the God debate finally, the latter are indifferent not only to Christianity but also to all religious inquiry and even 'curiosity' (*questionnement*). . . . This is the most radical form of detachment. It has eliminated not only the preliminary steps towards seeking God in a Christian environment—fundamental questioning (*questionnement*) is an integral co-ordinate in the existential process of the act of faith—but also the search (*quête*) for meaning which is a necessary condition for all religious or transcendental inquiry.'[3] For Johann Baptist Lotz, too,

86

professor of philosophy at the Gregorian, religious indifference is the most radical form of atheism: it is not atheism through negation, which still has to come to terms with affirmation, but atheism through insensibility: 'Nietzsche suffered terribly for his denial of God. However quite a few of our contemporaries live without God and do not feel they lack anything of capital importance. They are almost blind in regard to God, almost incapable of finding him, deprived of the faculty for him. It is a very serious thing, this atheism which consists of *insensibility* towards God.'[4]

Atheism and religious indifference—according to the sociologist Gianfranco Morra—are two phenomena which have the same matrix but correspond to two different characterisations: atheism conceals a deeply religious attitude, radical religious indifference reaches for the first time a total godlessness (*Gottlosigkeit*). We could say that religious indifference comes after atheism, not as a doctrine which implies further, more radical negations, but as an attitude and behaviour. Religious indifference is the calm possession on the existential level of an atheist position. Thus religious indifference seems to characterise—as Cardinal König puts it in the preface to the *Dossier* of the Secretariat, of which he is president—an epoch which is called post-religious and post-atheist. However, for the sociologist of religion, Antonio Grumelli, religious indifference occupies a middle position between religion and atheism, between affirmation and negation. But for Grumelli, too, religious indifference contains an implicit or practical judgment about the irrelevance of religion, which is total and of its nature definitive.

2. SECULARISATION AND RELIGIOUS INDIFFERENCE

Religious indifference as a mass phenomenon is a fact of modern society. Mircea Eliade writes: 'Even the great civilisations of the past have had a-religious people in them. It could easily be the case that they also existed in ancient times, although we do not have the documents to prove it. But only in modern Western society has the a-religious man come into his own.'[5]

In the Secretariat's *Dossier* Georges Cottier traces the development of indifference in religious matters from the time of the wars of religion until the threshold of our own century. The wars of religion saw the birth of *religious indifferentism*, which has not yet become the religious indifference of our own time, in that the former is indifference to the different doctrines of the various Christian denominations, whereas the latter is indifference to religion as such. From the historical reconstruction of this Swiss Dominican emerges the emblematic importance of two figures: Pascal and Comte: Comte as the antithesis of Pascal. For Pascal, faced with sceptical libertines, it is possible to give up the truth of science but not the search for saving truth; it is not possible not to care about salvation because everything is at stake: 'I can understand', he remarks in one of his *Thoughts*, 'not going deeply into the opinion of Copernicus, but as for this. . . ! It is important for my whole life to know whether the soul is mortal or immortal.'[6] For Comte on the other hand, the mind must rid itself of the chimera of religion and metaphysics; these occupied its infancy during which it tormented itself in vain with the insoluble question of *why*, and only ask *how* things are. In Pascalian terms, it is not saving truth which is interesting but, in fact, the opinion of Copernicus, or rather the knowledge of the universe which this gives us in view of a possible practical use: 'Know in order to foresee so that we can provide.'[7] The truth of religion and metaphysics passes into 'obsolescence'. What is of vital interest to Pascal becomes obsolete in the positivist view of Comte. This gives rise to the problem of the relation between a philosophical view and ethical and religious behaviour.

The social context is also important in the interpretation of the phenomenon of religious indifference. Antonio Grumelli's essay on the relationship between secularisation and indifference is one of the most illuminating in the whole *Dossier*. Secularisation is a complex phenomenon, and in religious terms, ambivalent. It may lie in continuity but also discontinuity and even opposition to the phenomenon of atheism. Continuity, because secularisation can be fertile ground for the growth of atheism. Discontinuity, in so far as secularisation causes the collapse of conventional and sociological religiosity and favours a renewal of religion on the personal and existential level: 'Secularisation may favour either the growth of atheist attitudes or the affirmation of a more mature and responsible religiosity.'[8] But also opposition, in that secularisation can also uproot those forms of atheism that are based on emotional reactions or are the result of social conditions, thereby preparing the ground for a possible religious commitment which is responsible and aware: 'Secularisation may be a double-edged sword which may fall upon either belief or unbelief. Its effects are unpredictable.'[9]

The ambivalence of the relationship between secularisation and atheism is reproduced in the relationship between secularisation and religious indifference. The aetiological factors of secularisation, viz., ideological pluralism, the increased demand for rationality and the process of industrialisation and urbanisation, create a crisis for shallow ideological positions, either of superficial religiousness or fashionable atheism, thereby favouring either the recovery of a responsible religious attitude or the shift to religious indifference: 'In a secularised society, religious indifference may, just as well have an atheist as a religious provenance.'[10]

3. FLIGHT INTO RELIGIOUS INDIFFERENCE?

But how can we explain the phenomenon of religious indifference from the anthropological-speculative point of view? We do not find new attempts to do so in the Secretariat's *Dossier* but we are referred to previous works on atheism, in particular those by Max Scheler, Karl Rahner, Johann Baptist Lotz and Georges Cottier.

For Max Scheler, the philosopher of values, it is not possible to choose between believing and not believing. Every consciousness has a sphere which is open to the Absolute, which may be occupied by the supreme Good or by a finite good which is pursued with 'infinite tension' and thus made absolute and transformed into an idol. The possibility of choice is restricted. 'The only possible choice', writes the Monacan philosopher in *Vom Ewigen des Menschen*, 'is that between having in the sphere of the absolute good which is adequate to the act of religion, viz., God, *or* having an idol.' Even the agnostic—Scheler uses this expression—believes in his way: 'In fact, the agnostic is not an unbeliever but a believer in nothing—he is a metaphysical nihilist. Believing in nothing is something completely different from not believing at all. 'Indifference is not a choice', concludes Wilhelm Keilback in support of Scheler, 'but a flight.'[11]

Rahner distinguishes between the transcendental plane open to the Absolute and the categorial and conceptual plane. A categorial atheist is not necessarily an atheist on the transcendental level. This distinction can also work with regard to religious indifference. The philosopher of the Gregorian University, Johann Baptist Lotz, has advanced the theory of levels of self-realisation. A person must find himself in order to find God and to the extent which he loses himself, he also loses God: 'Many people can no longer find themselves or can only reach very superficial layers of themselves. They cannot go deep inside themselves and this is where God's silent voice is heard.'

Georges Cottier distinguishes between nature, which is always directed towards God, and culture, which can become a second nature and may obscure the horizon open to transcendence. In his discussion of these attempts at explanation, Vincenzo Miano approaches this last solution.[12] As we see, the problem of religious indifference requires the working out of an adequate anthropology able to take into account the anthropological difference between believers and unbelievers.

4. PASTORAL CONSIDERATIONS

It is possible to discuss atheist arguments but it is much more difficult to deal with religious indifference, because there is nothing to hold on to. This means that the pastoral problems it presents are not simple and partly, they are new problems. The Secretariat's *Dossier* only suggests a few guidelines.

If religious indifference is a phenomenon of secular society and if secularisation is an overthrowing of the society's previous values, the Church's action should take the form of a massive educational operation to deepen the *discussion* of values and encourage the growth of awareness. The sociologist Antonio Grumelli writes: 'We are talking about a complex and constant educational work whose aim is to make people understand the role played by values in any society and particularly in our own. . . . This task becomes even more necessary when we realise that no proselytism today can work without a solid cultural base; it must operate not only on the organisational and emotional level but also and especially on the level of the values it upholds and to which it is trying to *convert* people.'[13] And the secretary general of the French episcopal conference, Gérard Defois, even suggests that 'cultural centres should be recognised as a sort of particular churches.'[14]

This difficult and urgent cultural work is what gives *witness* its importance, especially in secular society, in that it can act as a valid support to the preaching of values and as the only proper proof of this preaching. In a secular society with its ideological pluralism, every Christian must be willing to assume all his responsibilities. The witness of the laity to Christian values is essential. A clerical Church is not able to confront the problems caused by religious indifference, only a Christian community, within which communication and participation operate at the highest level.

The study of religious indifference produced by the Secretariat for Non-believers is a first attempt and as such only a beginning. Many problems are merely mentioned, such as the problem of a new religious language, of the credibility of the Church and its structures and the related problem of the ethical task of the Church not only as concerning individual morality but also the collective aspect of ethical problems. Other problems are not even mentioned and they must be faced or re-raised, problems such as the divisions between the Christian denominations, the pastoral problem of a brief formulation of the Christian message and the problem of nihilism, especially the 'full scale nihilism' which has finally taken leave of strong and absolute values.

Translated by Dinah Livingstone

Notes

1. In the vast four-volume work *L'ateismo contemporaneo* ed. G. Girardi (Turin 1967-9) there is no treatment of religious indifference. The editor of the work contributed a short article called 'Reflexions on religious indifference' to the issue of *Concilium* 23 devoted to 'Atheism and Indifference', 31.

2. *L'indifferenza religiosa* edited by the Secretariat for Non-believers (Rome 1978). (The volume was due out in 1975. Its publication was delayed for a few years for editorial reasons.)

3. A. Charron 'Les Divers types de distants. Essais de clarification' *Nouveau Dialogue* 11 (April 1975) 3-9.

4. J. B. Lotz 'L'ateismo come sfida ai cristiani' in *Psicologia dell' ateismo* (Rome 1967), p. 34.

5. M. Eliade *Il sacro e il profano* (Turin 1967) p. 159. (*The Sacred and the Profane; the nature of religion* (New York 1959)).

6. B. Pascal *Pensées* (Bibliotheque de la Pleiade 346, Paris 1954) p. 1181.

7. A. Comte *Lettres à Valat* (Letter of 28th September 1819).

8. *L'indifferenza religiosa*, cited in note 2, p. 92.

9. *Religione e ateismo nelle societá secolarizzate* ed. R. Caporale and A. Grumelli, (Bologna 1972), p. 60.

10. *L'indifferenza religiosa*, cited in note 2, p. 92.

11. See *ibid.* pp. 69-78.

12. See *ibid.* pp. 19-22.

13. *Ibid.* p. 94.

14. *Ibid.* p. 174.

Contributors

IGNACE BERTEN, OP, was born in 1940 in Brussels, Belgium, taught for several years at the International Institute Lumen Vitae and the Centre for Theological and Pastoral Studies in Brussels, and now works with the Cardinal Cardijn Seminary and the Justice and Peace Commission. His publications include *Histoire, révélation et foi. Dialogue avec Wolfhart Pannenberg* (1969) and *La Spirale de l'irresponsabilité . . .* (1978).

JEAN COLLET was born in 1932 and has been responsible for the cinema section of the journal *Etudes* since 1966. He teaches cinema and communications at the universities of Paris VII and Dijon and is programme adviser to the Institut National de l'Audio-Visual in Paris. M. Collet has published *Jean-Luc Godard* (1962 and 1973), *Le Cinéma en question* (1972) and *Le Cinéma de Francois Truffaut* (1977).

CLAUDE GEFFRÉ, OP, was born in Niort, France, in 1926. Having completed his philosophical and theological studies at the Dominican School of Le Saulchoir, he went on to teach dogma there and he occupied the post of Recteur des Facultés from 1965-1968. He has since then been teaching fundamental theology at the Institut Catholique in Paris, where he is also responsible for the doctoral cycle of studies. He is also editor in chief of the collection *Cogitatio Fidei* at the Editions du Cerf. Apart from numerous articles in various theological and pastoral journals, his most recent publications include the following: *Un nouvel âge de la théologie* (1972); *Un Espace pour Dieu* (1980); and, with others: *Procès de l'objectivé de Dieu* (1969); *Révélation de Dieu et language des hommes* (1972); *Herméneutique de la sécularisation* (1976); *Le Déplacement de la théologie* (1977); *La Révélation* (1977).

ROSINO GIBELLINI was born in Brescia, Italy, in 1926 and ordained priest in 1951. He gained a doctorate in theology at the Gregorian University, Rome, with a thesis on original sin and a doctorate in philosophy at the Catholic University, Milan, with a thesis on Teilhard de Chardin. Since 1965 he has been directing the theological programme of the Editrice Queriniana of Brescia which has been responsible for introducing to Italy the most significant currents of contemporary theology. Apart from editing several panoramic studies of contemporary theology in North and Latin America and of feminism in theology, he has himself published *La teologia de Jürgen Moltmann* (1975), *Teologia e ragione: Itinerario e opera di Wolfhart Pannenberg* (1980) and *Teilhard de Chardin: l'opera e le interpretatzioni* ([2]1981).

ROBERT KRESS, currently associate professor in the department of theology at the Catholic University of America, Washington, DC, USA, was born in 1932 at Jasper, Indiana, studied at St Meinrad, Innsbruck, Paris, Rome, University of Notre Dame, was a Visiting Fellow at Princeton Theological Seminary and Brown University and has degrees in philosophy, theology and education. He has published many articles in scholarly and popular journals. Among his books are *Whither Womankind* (Outstanding Book of the Year award from the College Theology Society 1976), *A Rahner Handbook* (1981), *The Difference That Jesus Makes* (1982), *The Church: Communion,*

Sacrament, Communication (1982) and *Touching the Divine: An Introduction to the Sacraments* (1983).

WILLY OBRIST was born in Switzerland in 1918, and studied philosophy and medicine before being trained as an analyst. He is a psychiatrist in private practice and teaches at the C. J. Jung Institute in Zurich. He has published *Die Mutation des Bewusstseits von archaischen zum heutigen Sebst- und Weltverständnis* (1980).

HEINZ ROBERT SCHLETTE, born in 1931 in Wesel on the lower Rhine, did philosophy, theology and religious studies at Münster and Munich with degrees in philosophy and theology. He gained his *Habilitation* in philosophy at Saarbrücken and since 1980 has been professor of philosophy at Bonn. His works include: *Aporie und Glaube* (1970); *Skeptische Religions-philosophie* (1972); *Albert Camus—Welt und Revolte* (1980); *Glaube und Distanz. Theologische Bemühungen um die Frage, wie man im Christentum bleiben könne* (1981). He is a frequent contributor to *Orientierung*.

JACQUES SOMMET, SJ, was born in Lyons, France, in 1912. Between 1962 and 1979 he served first as professor then as principal of the Jesuit Faculty of Philosophy in France. He has also been principal of the Centre d'Etudes et de Recherche d'action sociale. He edits *Incroyance et Foi*, the organ of the 'Service Incroyance-Foi', of which he is national secretary. He has written many articles, for a variety of publications, on political and social subjects, on atheism and unbelief, and on social philosophy.

JOSEPH J. SPAE, CICM, was born at Lochristi, Belgium, in 1913, and he studied orientalism and Buddhism at Leuven, Peking, Kyoto and Columbia University, New York, where he obtained a doctorate in Far Eastern languages and philosophy. He founded the Oriens Institute for Religious Research in Tokyo. In 1972-1976, he served as General Secretary of Sodepax in Rome and Geneva. At present he is consultor of the Vatican Secretariat for Non-Christians, director of the Chicago Institute of Theology and Culture, and editor of the quarterly *China Update*. His books include: *Itō Jinsai* (Peking 1948 and New York 1968); *Christian Corridors to Japan* (1968); *Christianity Encounters Japan* (1968); *Japanese Religiosity* (1971); *Shinto Man* (1972); and *Buddhist-Christian Empathy* (1980), all published by the Oriens Institute, Tokyo.

ANTON WEILER was born in the Netherlands in 1927. He studied philosophy and history at Nijmegen University and has been professor of medieval history since 1964 and of the philosophy of history since 1965 at Nijmegen. He is married and has five children. He has written many articles and the following books: *Heinrich von Gorkum (1431). Seine Stellung in der Philosophie und der Theologie des Spätmittelalters* (1962); *Geschiedenis van de kerk in Nederland* (1963) (together with O. J. de Jong, L. J. Rogier and C. W. Mönnich); *Deus in Terris. Middeleeuwse wortels van de totalitaire ideologie* (1965); *Necrologie, Kroniek en cartularium cum annexis van het fraterhuis te Doesburg (1432-1559)* (1974); *Christelijk bestaan in een seculaire cultuur* (1969) (together with others); *Monasticon Windeshemense 3: Niederlande* (1980) (together with Noël Geirnaert).

CONCILIUM

All back issues are still in print and available for sale. Orders should be sent to the publishers,

T. & T. CLARK LIMITED
36 George Street, Edinburgh EH2 2LQ, Scotland